Basic Guide to Programming Languages
Python, JavaScript, and Ruby

Kiet Huynh

Table of Contents

CHAPTER I
Introduction to Programming

1.1 What is Programming?

Programming, also known as coding, is the art of giving instructions to a computer to perform specific tasks. It involves writing sets of commands or instructions in a programming language that the computer can understand and execute. Programming lies at the heart of modern technology and is the foundation of software development, web development, data analysis, artificial intelligence, and more.

1.1.1 Why is Programming Important?

Programming is essential in today's digital age as it enables us to create software and applications that power our daily lives. From simple mobile apps to complex systems, programming drives innovation and automates tasks, making our lives more efficient and convenient.

For example, programming is used in web development to build interactive websites and web applications. Social media platforms, e-commerce websites, and online banking systems are all products of programming. In mobile app development, programming languages are used to create applications for smartphones and tablets, providing users with entertainment, productivity tools, and communication platforms.

In the field of data analysis and artificial intelligence, programming allows us to process and analyze vast amounts of data, uncover patterns, and make data-driven decisions. Machine learning and deep learning algorithms are also built using programming languages to develop intelligent systems that can learn and improve over time.

1.1.2 Getting Started with Programming

If you're new to programming, getting started can seem overwhelming, but don't worry – it's an exciting journey! Here are some steps to help you begin:

1. Choose a Programming Language: There are numerous programming languages to choose from, each with its own strengths and applications. Python, JavaScript, and Ruby are beginner-friendly languages with versatile applications, making them excellent choices for newcomers.

2. Set Up Your Development Environment: Once you've selected a programming language, you'll need to set up your development environment. This includes installing the necessary software, such as a code editor and a compiler or interpreter.

3. Learn the Basics: Begin with the fundamental concepts of programming, such as variables, data types, control structures (if statements, loops), and functions. These concepts form the building blocks of every program.

4. Practice, Practice, Practice: Programming is a skill that improves with practice. Start with small projects and gradually increase the complexity as you gain confidence.

5. Seek Help and Resources: There are plenty of online resources, tutorials, and coding communities available to support your learning journey. Don't hesitate to ask questions and seek guidance from experienced programmers.

1.1.3 Examples of Programming in Real Life

Let's explore some real-life examples of how programming is used in various fields:

1. Social Media Platforms: Social media websites like Facebook, Twitter, and Instagram rely heavily on programming to handle user interactions, store and retrieve data, and display content.

2. E-commerce Websites: Online shopping platforms such as Amazon and eBay use programming to manage product listings, shopping carts, payment processing, and order fulfillment.

3. Mobile Applications: Mobile apps, whether for entertainment, productivity, or utility, are created using programming languages to provide users with a seamless experience.

4. Data Analysis and Visualization: Data scientists and analysts use programming to process large datasets, perform statistical analysis, and create visualizations to gain insights from the data.

5. Artificial Intelligence and Machine Learning: The development of AI-powered chatbots, virtual assistants, and recommendation systems involves sophisticated programming techniques and algorithms.

6. Video Games: The gaming industry relies on programming to create realistic graphics, interactive gameplay, and immersive experiences for players.

In conclusion, programming is an invaluable skill that drives technological advancements and empowers us to shape the digital world. It's a creative and problem-solving endeavor that opens doors to exciting career opportunities and enables us to bring our ideas to life through software and applications. So, if you're eager to embark on an adventure into the world of programming, Chapter 1 is just the beginning of your exciting journey. Happy coding!

1.2. Why Learn Multiple Programming Languages?

Learning multiple programming languages offers several advantages that can enhance your programming skills, expand your career opportunities, and make you a more versatile and effective programmer. Each programming language has its strengths and weaknesses, and by learning different languages, you can leverage the unique features of each to tackle various tasks and challenges. In this section, we will explore the reasons why learning multiple programming languages is beneficial and how you can approach learning them.

1. Advantages of Learning Multiple Programming Languages:

1.1 Versatility: Different programming languages are suitable for different tasks. For instance, Python is known for its simplicity and readability, making it an excellent choice for beginners and for tasks involving data analysis and automation. On the other hand, JavaScript is commonly used for web development and allows you to create interactive and dynamic web applications. By learning both Python and JavaScript, you can work on a wider range of projects and adapt to different development environments.

1.2 Problem Solving: Each programming language has its own paradigms and approaches to problem-solving. Learning multiple languages exposes you to different programming paradigms such as procedural, object-oriented, and functional programming. This exposure enhances your ability to analyze problems from different perspectives and choose the most appropriate approach to tackle them.

1.3 Employability: Job markets often require knowledge of specific programming languages. By learning multiple languages, you become a more attractive candidate for a variety of job opportunities. For example, if you are proficient in Python and C++, you can apply for positions in data science, software development, or embedded systems engineering.

1.4 Understanding Legacy Code: In the professional world, you may encounter projects that involve maintaining or modifying legacy code written in older languages. Having knowledge of multiple programming languages makes it easier to understand and work with existing codebases.

1.5 Career Growth: As you progress in your programming career, you may take on roles that require expertise in specific languages or technologies. Learning multiple languages positions you for career growth, allowing you to move into specialized roles or leadership positions.

2. How to Learn Multiple Programming Languages:

2.1 Choose Your First Language Wisely: Start with a beginner-friendly language that is widely used and has a supportive community. Python is an excellent choice for beginners due to its readability and extensive libraries.

2.2 Master the Fundamentals: Before moving on to another language, ensure you have a solid understanding of programming fundamentals like variables, loops, functions, and data structures. A strong foundation will make learning new languages easier.

2.3 Practice Projects: Apply your knowledge by working on projects that interest you. Building real-world applications allows you to see how programming languages are used in practical scenarios.

2.4 Take Advantage of Online Resources: There are abundant online tutorials, courses, and coding platforms where you can learn new languages. Websites like Codecademy, Coursera, and Udemy offer courses on various programming languages.

2.5 Learn from Documentation: Each language has official documentation that provides in-depth information and examples. Reading the documentation is a great way to gain insights into the language's features and best practices.

2.6 Collaborate with Others: Join coding communities or attend programming meetups to collaborate with other learners and experienced developers. Participating in group projects can accelerate your learning and expose you to different perspectives.

2.7 Compare and Contrast: As you learn multiple languages, compare their syntax, features, and use cases. Understand how they solve similar problems differently and recognize their strengths and limitations.

3. Examples of Learning Multiple Programming Languages:

3.1 Full-Stack Web Developer: A full-stack web developer may need to work with multiple languages such as JavaScript, Python, and SQL. JavaScript is used for front-end development, Python for back-end, and SQL for database management.

3.2 Data Scientist: Data scientists often use Python for data manipulation and analysis due to its rich ecosystem of libraries like Pandas and NumPy. They may also use R for statistical analysis and visualization.

3.3 Game Developer: A game developer may use C++ for performance-critical parts of the game, Python for scripting, and JavaScript for web-based games or interactive elements.

In conclusion, learning multiple programming languages is a valuable investment in your programming career. It allows you to adapt to diverse projects, technologies, and job opportunities. By building a strong foundation in one language and gradually exploring others, you can become a well-rounded programmer capable of solving a wide range of problems. Embrace the journey of learning, and the programming world will become your oyster. Happy coding!

1.3. Choosing the Right Language for Your Projects

When starting a new programming project, one of the critical decisions you need to make is choosing the right programming language. Each programming language has its own strengths, weaknesses, and areas of application. Selecting the most suitable language for your project can significantly impact its success and your development experience. In this section, we will explore the factors to consider when choosing a programming language and provide practical guidance to help you make informed decisions.

1. Project Requirements and Goals:

Before diving into a specific language, it is essential to understand the requirements and goals of your project. Ask yourself the following questions:

1.1 What is the nature of the project? Is it a web application, desktop software, mobile app, data analysis, or a game?

1.2 What are the performance requirements? Does the project involve real-time processing, high-speed computations, or handling large datasets?

1.3 What are the scalability requirements? Will the project need to handle a growing number of users or data over time?

1.4 What platforms does the project need to support? Consider whether the application needs to run on Windows, macOS, Linux, or mobile platforms like iOS and Android.

1.5 Are there any external dependencies or existing systems that require integration?

1.6 What is your team's expertise? Consider the language proficiency of your team members to ensure efficient development and maintenance.

2. Popular Programming Languages and Their Use Cases:

2.1 Python: Python is a versatile and beginner-friendly language known for its readability and clean syntax. It is widely used in web development, scientific computing, data analysis, artificial intelligence, and automation. Django and Flask are popular Python frameworks for web development.

Example: If you are building a web application with complex data analysis features, Python might be a suitable choice.

2.2 JavaScript: JavaScript is a fundamental language for web development, enabling dynamic and interactive user interfaces. It is commonly used in front-end development with frameworks like React, Angular, or Vue.js.

Example: If you are creating a modern web application with real-time updates and interactive features, JavaScript is essential.

2.3 Java: Java is a powerful, platform-independent language used in enterprise-level applications, Android app development, and large-scale systems.

Example: If you are developing a mobile app for Android or a complex enterprise system, Java is a reliable choice.

2.4 C++: C++ is known for its performance and is widely used in systems programming, game development, and resource-intensive applications.

Example: If you are building a high-performance game or working on an operating system component, C++ might be a suitable option.

2.5 Swift: Swift is Apple's programming language for iOS and macOS app development. It is designed for safety, performance, and ease of use.

Example: If you are developing an iOS or macOS application, Swift is the primary language to consider.

2.6 Ruby: Ruby is renowned for its simplicity and readability, making it a popular choice for web development with the Ruby on Rails framework.

Example: If you are building a web application with rapid development requirements, Ruby on Rails can be a productive choice.

3. Considerations for Language Learning Curve:

Keep in mind the learning curve associated with each language, especially if you are new to programming. Some languages, like Python and JavaScript, have beginner-friendly syntax and extensive learning resources, making them great choices for beginners. On the other hand, languages like C++ and Rust may have steeper learning curves due to their complex syntax and memory management.

4. Community and Ecosystem:

Consider the size and activity of the language's community and ecosystem. A robust community means more learning resources, libraries, frameworks, and active support forums. A vibrant ecosystem can significantly streamline your development process.

5. Testing and Debugging Capabilities:

Ensure that the language supports proper testing and debugging tools. Effective testing and debugging are crucial for maintaining code quality and identifying and fixing issues quickly.

6. Long-term Maintenance:

Think about the long-term maintenance and support of the project. Choose a language with strong community support and longevity to ensure you can find developers and resources for maintenance in the future.

In conclusion, selecting the right programming language for your projects requires thoughtful consideration of the project's requirements, goals, team expertise, and the specific use cases of popular languages. Keep in mind that there is no one-size-fits-all language, and the best choice may vary depending on the unique aspects of your project. By carefully evaluating your options and understanding the strengths and weaknesses of each language, you can make an informed decision that sets your project up for success. Happy coding!

CHAPTER II
Getting Started with Python

2.1 Installing Python and Setting Up Development Environment

Python is a powerful and versatile programming language widely used for various applications, including web development, data analysis, artificial intelligence, and more. To begin your journey with Python, the first step is to install Python on your computer and set up a development environment. In this section, we will guide you through the process of installing Python and configuring your environment on different operating systems.

1. Installing Python:

Python is available for various operating systems, including Windows, macOS, and Linux. The latest stable version of Python can be downloaded from the official website (https://www.python.org/downloads/). Follow these steps to install Python on your system:

1.1 For Windows:

- Download the latest Python installer for Windows.

- Run the installer, and during the installation, make sure to check the option "Add Python X.X to PATH" (where X.X represents the version number).

- Click "Install Now" to complete the installation.

1.2 For macOS:

- macOS typically comes with a pre-installed version of Python. However, it is recommended to use the latest version of Python from the official website.

- Download the macOS installer, and run it to install Python.

1.3 For Linux:

- Most Linux distributions come with Python pre-installed. However, you can use the package manager to install Python if needed.

- Open the terminal and use the package manager specific to your Linux distribution to install Python.

2. Verifying the Installation:

After installing Python, you can verify the installation by opening a command prompt (Windows) or terminal (macOS and Linux) and typing the following command:

```
python --version
```

This command will display the installed Python version, confirming that Python is correctly installed.

3. Setting Up Development Environment:

To effectively work with Python, it is essential to set up a development environment. This involves using a code editor or Integrated Development Environment (IDE) that supports Python development. Some popular options include:

3.1 Visual Studio Code (VS Code):

- VS Code is a free and lightweight code editor that supports Python development through extensions.

- Install the Python extension from the VS Code marketplace to enable Python-specific features.

3.2 PyCharm:

- PyCharm is a powerful and user-friendly IDE specifically designed for Python development.

- Download and install the community edition of PyCharm, which is free and suitable for most Python projects.

3.3 Jupyter Notebook:

- Jupyter Notebook is an interactive computing environment that allows you to create and share documents containing live code, equations, visualizations, and narrative text.

- Install Jupyter Notebook using pip, the Python package manager:

```
pip install jupyterlab
```

4. Writing Your First Python Program:

Now that you have Python installed and your development environment set up, it's time to write your first Python program. A classic "Hello, World!" program is often used to demonstrate the basic syntax of a programming language. Open your code editor or IDE and create a new Python file with the extension ".py".

```python
# hello_world.py
print("Hello, World!")
```

Save the file and run it from the command line:

```
python hello_world.py
```

You should see the output "Hello, World!" displayed in the terminal.

Congratulations! You have successfully installed Python, set up your development environment, and written your first Python program. You are now ready to explore the endless possibilities of Python and delve into more complex projects. Happy coding!

2.2. Understanding Variables and Data Types

In Python, variables are used to store data values. They act as containers that hold different types of information, such as numbers, text, or collections of data. Before we dive into understanding variables, let's explore the different data types available in Python.

1. Numeric Data Types:

Python supports several numeric data types to represent numbers:

1.1 Integers (int): Integers are whole numbers, either positive or negative, without any fractional parts. For example:

```python
x = 10
y = -5
```

1.2 Floating-Point Numbers (float): Floating-point numbers are numbers with decimal points, allowing for fractional values. For example:

```python
pi = 3.14
salary = 1250.50
```

1.3 Complex Numbers (complex): Complex numbers consist of a real part and an imaginary part expressed as "real + imaginaryj". For example:

```python
```

```
z = 3 + 2j
```

2. Text Data Type:

In Python, text is represented using the "str" data type, which stands for "string". Strings are sequences of characters enclosed in single or double quotes. For example:

```python
name = 'John'
message = "Hello, Python!"
```

3. Boolean Data Type:

Boolean values represent two states: True or False. They are useful for making decisions in programming, such as in conditional statements and loops. For example:

```python
is_student = True
is_passed = False
```

4. Collection Data Types:

Python provides several collection data types to store multiple values.

4.1 Lists: Lists are ordered and mutable collections that can hold different data types. Elements are enclosed in square brackets and separated by commas. For example:

```python
numbers = [1, 2, 3, 4, 5]
names = ['Alice', 'Bob', 'Charlie']
```

4.2 Tuples: Tuples are similar to lists, but they are immutable, meaning their elements cannot be changed after creation. Tuples are enclosed in parentheses. For example:

```python
coordinates = (10, 20)
colors = ('red', 'green', 'blue')
```

4.3 Sets: Sets are unordered collections that contain unique elements. They are useful for performing mathematical operations like union, intersection, etc. Sets are defined using curly braces. For example:

```python
fruits = {'apple', 'banana', 'orange'}
```

4.4 Dictionaries: Dictionaries are key-value pairs, where each value is associated with a unique key. They are defined using curly braces, with each key-value pair separated by a colon. For example:

```python
student = {'name': 'John', 'age': 20, 'major': 'Computer Science'}
```

5. Type Conversion:

Python allows converting variables from one data type to another. You can use built-in functions like "int()", "float()", "str()", etc., for type conversion. For example:

```python
x = 10
y = float(x)
name = 'Alice'
age = str(25)
```

Understanding data types and variables is fundamental to Python programming. They form the basis for performing operations, making decisions, and building complex data structures. Practice using different data types and variables in your Python programs to gain a deeper understanding of their behavior and capabilities.

2.3. Working with Lists and Tuples

Lists and tuples are essential data structures in Python that allow you to store multiple values in a single variable. They are versatile and commonly used for various tasks like storing collections of items, iterating through data, and modifying elements. In this section, we will explore how to work with lists and tuples in Python.

1. Lists:

1.1 Creating Lists:

To create a list in Python, enclose the elements in square brackets and separate them with commas. Lists can hold different data types, and the elements can be added, removed, or modified after creation. For example:

```python
fruits = ['apple', 'banana', 'orange', 'grape']

numbers = [1, 2, 3, 4, 5]

mixed_list = ['Alice', 25, True]
```

1.2 Accessing Elements:

You can access individual elements of a list using their index. Remember that Python uses zero-based indexing, where the first element has an index of 0. For example:

```python
print(fruits[0])  # Output: 'apple'

print(numbers[2])  # Output: 3
```

1.3 Slicing Lists:

You can extract a portion of a list using slicing. Slicing allows you to specify a start and end index, and it returns a new list containing the elements within that range. For example:

```python
print(fruits[1:3])  # Output: ['banana', 'orange']

print(numbers[:3])  # Output: [1, 2, 3]

print(mixed_list[1:])  # Output: [25, True]
```

1.4 Modifying Elements:

Lists are mutable, so you can modify their elements after creation. Use the index to access the element you want to change and then assign a new value to it. For example:

```python
fruits[2] = 'kiwi'

print(fruits)  # Output: ['apple', 'banana', 'kiwi', 'grape']
```

1.5 Adding and Removing Elements:

You can add elements to a list using the "append()" method, which adds the element to the end of the list. To insert an element at a specific index, use the "insert()" method. To remove an element, use the "remove()" method, passing the element's value to be removed. For example:

```python
fruits.append('pear')

print(fruits)  # Output: ['apple', 'banana', 'kiwi', 'grape', 'pear']


fruits.insert(1, 'cherry')

print(fruits)  # Output: ['apple', 'cherry', 'banana', 'kiwi', 'grape', 'pear']


fruits.remove('kiwi')

print(fruits)  # Output: ['apple', 'cherry', 'banana', 'grape', 'pear']
```

1.6 List Methods:

Python provides various built-in methods to manipulate lists. Some useful methods include "pop()", which removes and returns the element at a specified index, "clear()", which removes all elements from the list, "count()", which counts the occurrences of a specific element, and "sort()", which sorts the list in ascending order. For example:

```python
numbers.pop(2)
print(numbers)  # Output: [1, 2, 4, 5]


numbers.clear()
print(numbers)  # Output: []


fruits_count = fruits.count('apple')
print(fruits_count)  # Output: 1


fruits.sort()
print(fruits)  # Output: ['apple', 'banana', 'cherry', 'grape', 'pear']
```

2. Tuples:

2.1 Creating Tuples:

Tuples are similar to lists, but they are immutable, meaning their elements cannot be changed after creation. Tuples are defined using parentheses and can hold different data types. For example:

```python
coordinates = (10, 20)
colors = ('red', 'green', 'blue')
```

2.2 Accessing Elements:

You can access elements in a tuple using their index, just like with lists. However, since tuples are immutable, you cannot modify their elements. For example:

```python
print(coordinates[0]) # Output: 10

print(colors[2]) # Output: 'blue'
```

2.3 Tuple Packing and Unpacking:

You can "pack" multiple values into a tuple by separating them with commas. Similarly, you can "unpack" a tuple into individual variables. This feature allows for convenient simultaneous assignment of variables. For example:

```python
person = ('John', 25, 'Engineer')

name, age, occupation = person

print(name) # Output: 'John'

print(age)  # Output: 25

print(occupation) # Output: 'Engineer'
```

2.4 Use Cases for Lists and Tuples:

- Lists are ideal for scenarios where you need to modify the elements or have a dynamic collection of items.

- Tuples are suitable for situations where the data should remain constant and not change during the program's execution.

Understanding how to work with lists and tuples is crucial for Python development. They enable you to manage and manipulate collections of data efficiently, making your programs more powerful and flexible. Practice using lists and tuples in your Python code to become comfortable with their functionality and explore their various applications.

2.4. Dictionaries and Sets: Managing Key-Value Pairs

Dictionaries and sets are essential data structures in Python that allow you to work with key-value pairs and unique elements, respectively. They are powerful tools for organizing and managing data efficiently. In this section, we will explore how to work with dictionaries and sets in Python.

1. Dictionaries:

1.1 Creating Dictionaries:

A dictionary is a collection of key-value pairs enclosed in curly braces {}. Each key-value pair is separated by a colon (:), and individual pairs are separated by commas. Keys must be unique and immutable (strings, numbers, or tuples), while values can be of any data type. For example:

```python
person = {
    'name': 'John',
    'age': 30,
    'occupation': 'Engineer'
}
```

1.2 Accessing and Modifying Values:

You can access the value associated with a specific key by using the key inside square brackets. If the key exists, the corresponding value is returned. For example:

```python
print(person['name'])  # Output: 'John'

print(person['age'])   # Output: 30
```

To modify the value associated with a key, simply assign a new value to the key. For example:

```python
person['age'] = 31

print(person['age'])  # Output: 31
```

1.3 Adding and Removing Key-Value Pairs:

You can add new key-value pairs to a dictionary by simply assigning a value to a new key. To remove a key-value pair, you can use the "del" keyword followed by the dictionary name and the key you want to remove. For example:

```python
person['city'] = 'New York'

print(person)  # Output: {'name': 'John', 'age': 31, 'occupation': 'Engineer', 'city': 'New York'}


del person['occupation']

print(person)  # Output: {'name': 'John', 'age': 31, 'city': 'New York'}
```

1.4 Dictionary Methods:

Python provides various built-in methods to manipulate dictionaries. Some useful methods include "keys()", which returns a list of all the keys, "values()", which returns a list of all the values, "items()", which returns a list of all the key-value pairs as tuples, and "get()", which retrieves the value associated with a key, with an option to provide a default value if the key is not found. For example:

```python
print(person.keys())   # Output: dict_keys(['name', 'age', 'city'])

print(person.values()) # Output: dict_values(['John', 31, 'New York'])

print(person.items())  # Output: dict_items([('name', 'John'), ('age', 31), ('city', 'New York')])


occupation = person.get('occupation', 'Unemployed')

print(occupation)  # Output: 'Unemployed'
```

2. Sets:

2.1 Creating Sets:

A set is an unordered collection of unique elements enclosed in curly braces {}. Sets are used when you want to eliminate duplicate values from a collection or check membership quickly. For example:

```python
fruits = {'apple', 'banana', 'orange', 'apple'}

print(fruits) # Output: {'apple', 'banana', 'orange'} (Note that 'apple' appears only once)
```

2.2 Working with Sets:

Sets support various mathematical set operations, such as union, intersection, difference, and symmetric difference. You can perform these operations using built-in methods or operators. For example:

```python
set1 = {1, 2, 3}
set2 = {3, 4, 5}


union_set = set1.union(set2)
print(union_set)  # Output: {1, 2, 3, 4, 5}


intersection_set = set1.intersection(set2)
print(intersection_set)  # Output: {3}


difference_set = set1.difference(set2)
print(difference_set)  # Output: {1, 2}


symmetric_difference_set = set1.symmetric_difference(set2)
print(symmetric_difference_set)  # Output: {1, 2, 4, 5}
```


2.3 Set Methods:

Python provides various built-in methods for sets. Some useful methods include "add()", which adds an element to the set, "remove()", which removes an element from the set (raises an error if the element is not found), and "discard()", which removes an element from the set (no error if the element is not found). For example:

```python
fruits.add('pear')
print(fruits)  # Output: {'apple', 'banana', 'orange', 'pear'}


fruits.remove('banana')
print(fruits)  # Output: {'apple', 'orange', 'pear'}


fruits.discard('kiwi')  # No error even if 'kiwi' is not in the set
```

Understanding dictionaries and sets is crucial for managing data effectively in Python. They provide powerful capabilities for organizing and manipulating data, and their uniqueness and efficiency

 make them essential tools in many programming scenarios. Practice working with dictionaries and sets to become proficient in using them in your Python projects.

2.5. Conditional Statements: Making Decisions

Conditional statements, also known as control structures, allow Python programs to make decisions and perform different actions based on specific conditions. These statements form the foundation for building dynamic and responsive programs. In this section, we will explore conditional statements in Python and understand how to use them effectively.

1. If Statement:

The most basic form of a conditional statement is the "if" statement. It allows the program to execute a block of code only if a certain condition is true. The syntax for the "if" statement is as follows:

```python
if condition:

    # code block to execute if the condition is true

```

For example, consider a program that checks whether a given number is positive or negative:

```python
num = -5


if num > 0:

    print("The number is positive.")

```

In this example, if the value of "num" is greater than 0, the message "The number is positive." will be printed.

2. If-Else Statement:

The "if-else" statement allows the program to execute one block of code if a condition is true and another block of code if the condition is false. The syntax for the "if-else" statement is as follows:

```python
if condition:
```

```
    # code block to execute if the condition is true
else:

    # code block to execute if the condition is false
```

Continuing with the previous example, we can modify it to include an "if-else" statement to handle negative numbers:

```python
num = -5


if num > 0:

    print("The number is positive.")
else:

    print("The number is negative.")
```

In this case, if "num" is greater than 0, the message "The number is positive." will be printed, otherwise, "The number is negative." will be printed.

3. Elif Statement:

The "elif" statement, short for "else if," allows the program to check multiple conditions one by one and execute the code block associated with the first true condition. The syntax for the "elif" statement is as follows:

```python
if condition1:
```

```python
    # code block to execute if condition1 is true
elif condition2:
    # code block to execute if condition2 is true
elif condition3:
    # code block to execute if condition3 is true
# and so on...
else:
    # code block to execute if none of the conditions are true
```

Let's illustrate this with an example of grading students based on their scores:

```python
score = 85

if score >= 90:
    print("Grade: A")
elif score >= 80:
    print("Grade: B")
elif score >= 70:
    print("Grade: C")
elif score >= 60:
    print("Grade: D")
else:
    print("Grade: F")
```

```
```

In this example, the program will print the corresponding grade based on the value of "score."

4. Nested Conditional Statements:

Python allows you to nest conditional statements, which means you can have one conditional statement inside another. This allows for more complex decision-making in your programs. The syntax for nesting conditional statements is as follows:

```python
if condition1:
    # code block to execute if condition1 is true
    if condition2:
        # code block to execute if condition1 and condition2 are both true
    else:
        # code block to execute if condition1 is true but condition2 is false
else:
    # code block to execute if condition1 is false
```

Nested conditional statements can be helpful when you need to check multiple conditions with varying levels of complexity.

5. Logical Operators:

Logical operators (and, or, not) can be used to combine multiple conditions in a single conditional statement. They allow you to create more sophisticated condition checks. Here's how they work:

- "and" operator: The condition is true if both operands are true.

- "or" operator: The condition is true if at least one of the operands is true.

- "not" operator: This operator negates the condition, i.e., if the condition is true, "not" makes it false, and vice versa.

For example, let's modify our previous grading example using logical operators:

```python
score = 85

if score >= 90 and score <= 100:
    print("Grade: A")
elif score >= 80 and score < 90:
    print("Grade: B")
elif score >= 70 and score < 80:
    print("Grade: C")
elif score >= 60 and score < 70:
    print("Grade: D")
else:
    print("Grade: F")
```

In this example, we use the "and" operator to combine two conditions in each "if" statement.

6. Ternary Operator:

Python supports the ternary operator, which allows you to write conditional expressions in a single line. The syntax for the ternary operator is as follows:

```python
result = value_if_true if condition else value_if_false
```

Let's use the ternary operator to print the maximum of two numbers:

```python
num1 = 10
num2 = 15

max_num = num1 if num1 > num2 else num2
print("The maximum number is:", max_num)
```

In this example, the variable "max_num" will store the greater of the two numbers.

In conclusion, conditional statements in Python enable your programs to make decisions based on specific conditions. Understanding how to use "if," "if-else," "elif," and logical operators allows you to write more flexible and intelligent code. Practice using these statements in various scenarios to enhance your programming skills.

2.6. Loops: Iterating Through Data

Loops are an essential part of programming that allow us to execute a block of code repeatedly. They are particularly useful when dealing with collections of data, such as lists, strings, or dictionaries. In Python, there are two main types of loops: "for" loops and "while" loops. In this section, we will explore both types of loops and learn how to iterate through data effectively.

1. For Loops:

A "for" loop is used to iterate over a sequence, such as a list, string, or tuple. The loop will execute a specified block of code for each item in the sequence. The syntax for a "for" loop is as follows:

```python
for item in sequence:
    # code block to execute for each item in the sequence
```

For example, let's use a "for" loop to print each element of a list:

```python
fruits = ['apple', 'banana', 'orange']

for fruit in fruits:
    print(fruit)
```

This will output:

```
```

apple

banana

orange

```

## 2. Iterating Through a String:

Strings are sequences of characters, and we can use a "for" loop to iterate through each character in a string:

```python
message = "Hello, World!"

for char in message:
    print(char)
```

This will output each character of the string on a separate line.

3. Using the range() Function:

The range() function generates a sequence of numbers that can be used with a "for" loop to repeat an action a specific number of times. The syntax for the range() function is as follows:

```python
range(start, stop, step)
```
```

- start: The starting number of the sequence (inclusive).

- stop: The ending number of the sequence (exclusive).

- step: The increment between each number (default is 1).

For example, let's use a "for" loop with the range() function to print the first five even numbers:

```python
for num in range(0, 10, 2):
    print(num)
```

This will output:

```
0
2
4
6
8
```

4. While Loops:

A "while" loop is used to repeatedly execute a block of code as long as a certain condition is true. The loop will continue running until the condition becomes false. The syntax for a "while" loop is as follows:

```python
while condition:
    # code block to execute as long as the condition is true
```

For example, let's use a "while" loop to count down from 5 to 1:

```python
count = 5

while count > 0:
    print(count)
    count -= 1
```

This will output:

```
5
4
3
2
1
```

5. Loop Control Statements:

Python provides two loop control statements: "break" and "continue."

- "break" statement: It is used to exit the loop prematurely when a certain condition is met. For example:

```python
for num in range(1, 11):
    if num == 5:
        break
    print(num)
```

In this case, the loop will stop when "num" is equal to 5.

- "continue" statement: It is used to skip the current iteration of the loop and move to the next iteration. For example:

```python
for num in range(1, 11):
    if num == 5:
        continue
    print(num)
```

In this case, the number 5 will be skipped, and the loop will continue printing the other numbers.

6. Nested Loops:

Python allows us to nest loops, meaning we can have a loop inside another loop. This is useful for iterating through multiple levels of data. For example:

```python
rows = 3
cols = 3

for i in range(rows):
    for j in range(cols):
        print(f"({i}, {j})")
```

This will output all possible combinations of (i, j) for i = 0 to 2 and j = 0 to 2.

In conclusion, loops are powerful tools that allow us to process and manipulate data efficiently. By understanding "for" loops, "while" loops, and loop control statements, you can perform repetitive tasks with ease. Additionally, nested loops enable you to handle complex data structures. Practice using loops with different data types and scenarios to become proficient in Python's iteration capabilities.

2.7. Functions: Reusable Code Blocks

Functions are a fundamental concept in programming that allow us to break our code into reusable and modular blocks. They help organize code, make it easier to read and maintain, and promote code reusability. In Python, functions are defined using the "def" keyword followed by the function name, parentheses, and a colon. Any code inside the function is indented.

1. Creating Functions:

To define a function, use the following syntax:

```python
def function_name(parameters):
    # code block
    return result
```

- "function_name": A descriptive name for the function.
- "parameters": Optional input variables that the function can accept.
- "return": Optional statement to return a value from the function.

For example, let's create a function to calculate the area of a rectangle:

```python
def calculate_area(length, width):
    area = length * width
    return area
```

2. Calling Functions:

Once a function is defined, we can call it to execute the code inside it. To call a function, simply use its name followed by parentheses and any required arguments. For example:

```python
```

```
length = 5
width = 3
result = calculate_area(length, width)
print(result)
```

This will output:

```
15
```

3. Default Arguments:

Python allows us to set default values for function parameters. When a default value is provided, it becomes optional when calling the function. If no value is passed, the default value is used. For example:

```python
def greet(name="Guest"):
    print(f"Hello, {name}!")


greet()        # Output: Hello, Guest!
greet("John")  # Output: Hello, John!
```

4. Variable Scope:

Variables defined inside a function have local scope, which means they are only accessible within that function. On the other hand, variables defined outside a function have global scope and can be accessed both inside and outside functions. However, if a variable is modified inside a function without explicitly declaring it as global, Python will create a new local variable with the same name, leaving the global variable unchanged.

5. Lambda Functions:

Lambda functions, also known as anonymous functions, are short and simple functions defined using the "lambda" keyword. They are often used for small tasks and are not assigned a name like regular functions. The syntax for a lambda function is as follows:

```python
lambda arguments: expression
```

For example:

```python
add = lambda x, y: x + y
result = add(3, 5)
print(result)   # Output: 8
```

6. Recursion:

Recursion is a technique where a function calls itself to solve a problem. It is useful for solving problems that can be broken down into smaller sub-problems of the same type. However, it is essential to have a base case to stop the recursive calls; otherwise, the function will run indefinitely and lead to a stack overflow.

7. The "pass" Statement:

If you need to create a function's structure without implementing the code inside it, you can use the "pass" statement. It acts as a placeholder and prevents syntax errors. For example:

```python
def function_name():
    pass
```

In conclusion, functions are vital tools in Python that promote code organization, reusability, and readability. By understanding how to define functions, pass arguments, use default values, and handle variable scope, you can create powerful and modular code. Additionally, lambda functions provide a concise way to define simple functions on the fly. Recursion allows you to solve complex problems efficiently, and the "pass" statement helps you lay the groundwork for future code implementation. Practice creating and using functions to improve your Python programming skills and build robust applications.

2.8. Modules and Libraries: Extending Python's Capabilities

Python's strength lies not only in its simple syntax and ease of use but also in its extensive collection of modules and libraries that enhance its capabilities. These modules and libraries are pre-built code packages that provide additional functionality, allowing you to perform various tasks without reinventing the wheel. In this chapter, we will explore how to work with modules and libraries, including how to import them into your Python programs and leverage their power to streamline your code.

1. Importing Modules:

Python has a vast standard library that comes with the language by default. To use functions or classes from a module, you need to import it into your code. There are several ways to import modules:

a. Importing the Entire Module:

```python
import math
```

b. Importing Specific Functions or Classes:

```python
from math import sqrt, pi
```

c. Giving Modules an Alias:

```python
import numpy as np
```

2. Exploring Common Modules:

Python offers a wide range of standard modules for various purposes, such as math operations, file handling, date and time manipulation, and more. Some common modules include:

- `math`: Provides mathematical functions like `sqrt`, `sin`, `cos`, etc.

- `random`: Allows you to generate random numbers and make random selections.

- `os`: Provides operating system-related functionality like working with files and directories.

- `datetime`: Helps manipulate dates and times.

- `csv`: Facilitates reading and writing CSV files.

3. Installing External Libraries:

While Python's standard library is extensive, you can also install external libraries to extend its capabilities further. The Python Package Index (PyPI) is a repository of third-party libraries that you can install using the `pip` package manager. For example:

```bash
pip install requests
```

This command installs the `requests` library, which is commonly used for making HTTP requests.

4. Working with External Libraries:

Once you've installed an external library, you can import and use it in your code. For instance, the `requests` library is handy for making HTTP requests and working with APIs:

```python
import requests
```

```
response = requests.get("https://api.example.com/data")
if response.status_code == 200:

    data = response.json()

    print(data)
else:

    print("Failed to fetch data.")
```

5. Creating Custom Modules:

Besides using existing modules, you can create your own custom modules to organize your code into reusable pieces. To create a module, write your functions or classes in a `.py` file, and then import that file into other Python scripts.

6. Building Your Library of Functions:

As you gain experience in Python, you'll find yourself creating your own library of useful functions that can be reused in different projects. This personalized library will save you time and effort, allowing you to focus on solving unique challenges.

7. Exploring Popular Libraries:

Python's community has developed numerous powerful libraries for various domains, such as:

- `NumPy`: For numerical computations and working with arrays.

- `Pandas`: For data manipulation and analysis.

- `Matplotlib` and `Seaborn`: For data visualization.

- `Django` and `Flask`: For web development.

- `TensorFlow` and `PyTorch`: For machine learning and deep learning.

In conclusion, modules and libraries are integral to Python programming. They extend Python's capabilities, enabling you to perform complex tasks efficiently. By leveraging Python's standard library, installing external libraries, and creating custom modules, you can build powerful applications and explore a wide range of possibilities in Python. Additionally, exploring popular libraries will introduce you to specialized tools for data analysis, machine learning, web development, and more. Continuously expand your knowledge of Python's modules and libraries to become a proficient and versatile Python programmer.

CHAPTER III
Introduction to JavaScript

3.1 Setting Up the JavaScript Environment

JavaScript is a versatile and widely used programming language for web development. It allows you to add interactivity and dynamic content to web pages, making it an essential language for front-end web development. In this chapter, we will walk you through the process of setting up a JavaScript environment on your local machine so that you can start writing and executing JavaScript code.

1. Text Editors and Integrated Development Environments (IDEs):

To write JavaScript code, you need a text editor or an Integrated Development Environment (IDE). Some popular choices include:

- Visual Studio Code: A lightweight and powerful text editor with extensive JavaScript support.

- Sublime Text: A customizable and fast text editor suitable for JavaScript development.

- WebStorm: A feature-rich IDE specifically designed for web development.

Choose the one that best suits your needs and preferences. After installing your preferred text editor or IDE, you're ready to start writing JavaScript code.

2. Creating an HTML File:

Since JavaScript is often used in conjunction with HTML and CSS for web development, we will create an HTML file to link our JavaScript code. To do this, open your text editor or IDE, and create a new file with a `.html` extension. Here's a simple HTML structure:

```html
<!DOCTYPE html>
<html>
<head>
    <title>JavaScript Demo</title>
</head>
<body>
    <h1>Hello, JavaScript!</h1>
    <script src="app.js"></script>
</body>
</html>
```

3. Writing JavaScript Code:

Inside the same directory as your HTML file, create a new file named `app.js`. This file will contain your JavaScript code. Let's add a basic example to demonstrate JavaScript's interactivity:

```javascript
// app.js
alert("Welcome to JavaScript!");
```

```
let name = prompt("What's your name?");

console.log("Hello, " + name + "!");
```

In this example, we use the `alert` function to display a pop-up message when the web page loads. Then, we use the `prompt` function to ask the user for their name. Finally, we use `console.log` to print a personalized greeting message to the browser console.

4. Linking JavaScript to HTML:

To connect your `app.js` file to the HTML file, we use the `script` tag inside the `body` section of the HTML file:

```html
<script src="app.js"></script>
```

By doing this, the JavaScript code in `app.js` will be executed when the HTML page loads, and the user will see the welcome message and the prompt to enter their name.

5. Testing Your Code:

To test your JavaScript code, open the HTML file in your web browser. You should see the welcome message pop-up and a prompt asking for your name. After entering your name, open the browser console (usually accessible through Developer Tools), and you should see the personalized greeting printed in the console.

6. Exploring Browser Developer Tools:

Browser Developer Tools are essential for JavaScript development. They allow you to inspect, debug, and profile your code. Each browser has its own set of Developer Tools, but the common way to open them is by right-clicking on the web page and selecting "Inspect" or "Inspect Element." The Developer Tools typically have tabs for Elements, Console, Sources, and more. The Console tab is particularly useful for logging messages and debugging your JavaScript code.

7. Learning JavaScript Fundamentals:

With the basic setup and understanding of JavaScript, you can now explore its fundamental concepts, such as variables, data types, functions, loops, and conditional statements. These concepts are the building blocks of JavaScript, enabling you to create more complex and interactive web applications.

In conclusion, setting up the JavaScript environment is the first step to start your journey as a JavaScript developer. With a text editor or IDE, an HTML file, and a JavaScript file, you can begin writing and executing JavaScript code. The combination of JavaScript, HTML, and CSS is the backbone of web development, and learning JavaScript will open up numerous opportunities for you to create dynamic and engaging web applications. As you delve deeper into JavaScript, you'll discover its vast potential and how it empowers you to build modern web experiences. Happy coding!

3.2. Variables, Data Types, and Operators

In JavaScript, variables are used to store data that can be accessed and manipulated throughout your code. Understanding variables and data types is crucial as they form the foundation of any programming language. Additionally, operators allow you to perform various operations on data, enabling you to build complex logic and calculations in your code. In this section, we will explore variables, data types, and operators in JavaScript with practical examples.

1. Variables in JavaScript:

To declare a variable in JavaScript, use the `var`, `let`, or `const` keyword, followed by the variable name. Here's a simple example:

```javascript
var message;
let age;
const pi = 3.14;
```

- The `var` keyword declares a variable with function scope (pre-ES6).

- The `let` keyword declares a variable with block scope (ES6 and later).

- The `const` keyword declares a constant variable whose value cannot be changed after initialization.

2. Assigning Values to Variables:

You can assign values to variables using the assignment operator `=`. Here are some examples:

```javascript
var message = "Hello, JavaScript!";
let age = 25;
const pi = 3.14;
```

3. Data Types in JavaScript:

JavaScript has several data types, including:

- Primitive data types: `string`, `number`, `boolean`, `null`, `undefined`, and `symbol`.
- Complex data types: `object` and `function`.

Examples:

```javascript
var name = "John"; // string
var age = 30; // number
var isStudent = true; // boolean
var car = null; // null
var job; // undefined
```

4. Operators in JavaScript:

JavaScript supports various operators to perform operations on data:

- Arithmetic operators: `+`, `-`, `*`, `/`, `%` (modulus), `++`, and `--`.
- Assignment operators: `=`, `+=`, `-=`, `*=`, `/=`, and `%=`.

```javascript
var a = 10;
var b = 5;
var result = a + b; // 15
a += 2; // a is now 12
```

- Comparison operators: `==`, `!=`, `===`, `!==`, `>`, `<`, `>=`, and `<=`.

```javascript
var age = 18;
console.log(age == 18); // true
console.log(age !== "18"); // true (strict inequality)
```

- Logical operators: `&&` (AND), `||` (OR), and `!` (NOT).

```javascript
var isStudent = true;
var hasJob = false;
console.log(isStudent && hasJob); // false
console.log(isStudent || hasJob); // true
```

5. Type Conversion:

JavaScript performs automatic type conversion in certain situations. For example, adding a string to a number converts the number to a string:

```javascript
var x = 10;
var y = "5";
var result = x + y; // "105" (string concatenation)
```

You can also explicitly convert data types using built-in functions like `parseInt()` and `parseFloat()`:

```javascript
var strNumber = "10";
var intNumber = parseInt(strNumber); // 10 (converted to integer)
```

6. String Concatenation:

To concatenate strings, you can use the `+` operator:

```javascript
```

```javascript
var firstName = "John";

var lastName = "Doe";

var fullName = firstName + " " + lastName; // "John Doe"
```

7. Template Literals:

Template literals provide a more convenient way to work with strings, allowing you to embed variables directly within a string using backticks (`):

```javascript
var name = "Alice";

var message = `Hello, ${name}!`; // "Hello, Alice!"
```

In conclusion, understanding variables, data types, and operators is fundamental in JavaScript programming. Variables allow you to store and manipulate data, data types define the nature of the data, and operators enable you to perform operations on that data. As you practice and become more familiar with these concepts, you'll be better equipped to build more sophisticated and interactive applications. So, take your time to experiment with variables, explore different data types, and experiment with various operators to gain a solid understanding of JavaScript's core features. Happy coding!

3.3. Arrays: Storing and Manipulating Data

Arrays are an essential data structure in JavaScript that allow you to store multiple values in a single variable. They provide a way to manage and manipulate collections of data efficiently. In this section, we will explore arrays in detail, learn how to create and manipulate them, and understand various array methods to work with data effectively.

1. Creating Arrays:

To create an array in JavaScript, use square brackets `[]` and separate the elements with commas. Elements in an array can have different data types.

```javascript
var fruits = ["apple", "banana", "orange"];
var numbers = [1, 2, 3, 4, 5];
var mixedArray = [10, "hello", true];
```

2. Accessing Array Elements:

You can access individual elements of an array using their index. The index starts from 0 for the first element and increments by 1 for each subsequent element.

```javascript
var fruits = ["apple", "banana", "orange"];
console.log(fruits[0]); // "apple"
console.log(fruits[2]); // "orange"
```

3. Array Length:

The `length` property of an array returns the number of elements it contains.

```javascript
var fruits = ["apple", "banana", "orange"];
console.log(fruits.length); // 3
```

4. Modifying Array Elements:

You can modify array elements by assigning new values to specific indices.

```javascript
var fruits = ["apple", "banana", "orange"];
fruits[1] = "grape";
console.log(fruits); // ["apple", "grape", "orange"]
```

5. Adding and Removing Elements:

JavaScript provides several methods to add and remove elements from an array:

- `push()`: Adds one or more elements to the end of the array.

```javascript
var fruits = ["apple", "banana"];
fruits.push("orange", "grape");
console.log(fruits); // ["apple", "banana", "orange", "grape"]
```

- `pop()`: Removes the last element from the array and returns it.

```javascript
var fruits = ["apple", "banana", "orange"];
var removedElement = fruits.pop();
console.log(fruits); // ["apple", "banana"]
console.log(removedElement); // "orange"
```

- `unshift()`: Adds one or more elements to the beginning of the array.

```javascript
var fruits = ["apple", "banana"];
fruits.unshift("orange", "grape");
console.log(fruits); // ["orange", "grape", "apple", "banana"]
```

- `shift()`: Removes the first element from the array and returns it.

```javascript
var fruits = ["apple", "banana", "orange"];

var removedElement = fruits.shift();

console.log(fruits); // ["banana", "orange"]

console.log(removedElement); // "apple"
```

6. Array Methods:

JavaScript arrays come with a variety of built-in methods that make working with data more convenient:

- `indexOf()`: Returns the index of the first occurrence of a specified element.

```javascript
var fruits = ["apple", "banana", "orange"];

console.log(fruits.indexOf("banana")); // 1

console.log(fruits.indexOf("grape")); // -1 (not found)
```

- `splice()`: Adds or removes elements from an array at a specific index.

```javascript
var fruits = ["apple", "banana", "orange"];
```

```javascript
fruits.splice(1, 0, "grape"); // Add "grape" at index 1
console.log(fruits); // ["apple", "grape", "banana", "orange"]


fruits.splice(2, 1); // Remove 1 element at index 2
console.log(fruits); // ["apple", "grape", "orange"]
```

- `slice()`: Extracts a portion of an array and returns a new array.

```javascript
var fruits = ["apple", "banana", "orange", "grape"];
var citrusFruits = fruits.slice(1, 3);
console.log(citrusFruits); // ["banana", "orange"]
```

7. Iterating through Arrays:

You can use loops like `for` and `forEach()` to iterate through arrays and perform operations on each element.

- Using `for` loop:

```javascript
var fruits = ["apple", "banana", "orange"];
for (var i = 0; i < fruits.length; i++) {
```

```
    console.log(fruits[i]);

}
```

- Using `forEach()`:

```javascript
var fruits = ["apple", "banana", "orange"];
fruits.forEach(function (fruit) {
  console.log(fruit);
});
```

In conclusion, arrays are a powerful data structure in JavaScript that allow you to store and manipulate collections of data. You can create arrays, access and modify elements, add or remove elements, and use array methods for efficient data manipulation. Understanding how to work with arrays is essential for any JavaScript developer, as it forms the backbone of many programming tasks. Practice using arrays and explore various array methods to enhance your proficiency in JavaScript programming. Happy coding!

3.4. Objects and Classes: Creating Complex Data Structures

In JavaScript, objects and classes play a crucial role in creating complex data structures and organizing code. Objects are composite data types that allow you to store key-value pairs, while classes provide a blueprint for creating objects with shared properties and methods. Understanding objects and classes is essential for developing scalable and maintainable JavaScript applications. In this section, we will delve into objects, classes, and their usage in JavaScript.

1. Creating Objects:

In JavaScript, you can create objects using object literals or constructors.

- Object Literals:

Object literals are a convenient way to create objects by directly defining their properties and values.

```javascript
var person = {
  firstName: "John",
  lastName: "Doe",
  age: 30,
  sayHello: function() {
    console.log("Hello, I'm " + this.firstName + " " + this.lastName + ".");
  }
};
```

- Constructors and the `new` Keyword:

Constructors are functions that act as blueprints for creating objects. You can use the `new` keyword to create instances of objects from constructors.

```javascript
function Person(firstName, lastName, age) {
  this.firstName = firstName;
  this.lastName = lastName;
  this.age = age;
  this.sayHello = function() {
    console.log("Hello, I'm " + this.firstName + " " + this.lastName + ".");
  };
}


var person = new Person("John", "Doe", 30);
```

2. Accessing Object Properties and Methods:

You can access object properties and methods using dot notation or bracket notation.

```javascript
console.log(person.firstName); // "John"
console.log(person["lastName"]); // "Doe"
person.sayHello(); // "Hello, I'm John Doe."
```

3. Classes and Prototypes:

ES6 introduced class syntax, providing a more structured way to create objects. Under the hood, classes still use prototypes for inheritance.

- Class Declaration:

```javascript
class Person {
  constructor(firstName, lastName, age) {
    this.firstName = firstName;
    this.lastName = lastName;
    this.age = age;
  }

  sayHello() {
    console.log("Hello, I'm " + this.firstName + " " + this.lastName + ".");
  }
}
```

- Creating Objects from Classes:

```javascript
var person = new Person("John", "Doe", 30);
```

4. Inheritance with Classes:

Classes in JavaScript support inheritance through the `extends` keyword. Subclasses can inherit properties and methods from a parent class.

```javascript
class Employee extends Person {
  constructor(firstName, lastName, age, jobTitle) {
    super(firstName, lastName, age);
    this.jobTitle = jobTitle;
  }

  displayJobTitle() {
    console.log("Job Title: " + this.jobTitle);
  }
}

var employee = new Employee("Jane", "Smith", 25, "Software Engineer");
employee.sayHello(); // "Hello, I'm Jane Smith."
employee.displayJobTitle(); // "Job Title: Software Engineer"
```

5. Object Methods and `this` Keyword:

When defining methods inside objects or classes, the `this` keyword refers to the current instance of the object. It allows you to access and modify object properties within the methods.

```javascript
var person = {
  firstName: "John",
  lastName: "Doe",
  sayHello: function() {
    console.log("Hello, I'm " + this.firstName + " " + this.lastName + ".");
  }
};

person.sayHello(); // "Hello, I'm John Doe."
```

6. Object Destructuring:

Destructuring is a convenient way to extract object properties and assign them to variables.

```javascript
var person = {
  firstName: "John",
  lastName: "Doe",
  age: 30
};
```

```javascript
// Object Destructuring
var { firstName, lastName, age } = person;

console.log(firstName); // "John"
console.log(lastName); // "Doe"
console.log(age); // 30
```
```

In conclusion, objects and classes are essential concepts in JavaScript for creating complex data structures and organizing code. Objects allow you to group related data and behavior together, while classes provide a blueprint for creating objects with shared properties and methods. Understanding how to work with objects and classes will enable you to build more maintainable and scalable JavaScript applications. Practice creating objects and defining classes with various functionalities to enhance your proficiency in JavaScript programming. Happy coding!

## 3.5. Conditional Statements and Loops in JavaScript

Conditional statements and loops are fundamental programming constructs that enable you to control the flow of your code and perform repetitive tasks efficiently. In JavaScript, these features play a crucial role in decision-making and iterating through data. In this section, we will explore conditional statements and different types of loops in JavaScript.

**1. Conditional Statements:**

Conditional statements allow your code to make decisions based on certain conditions. The most common conditional statement in JavaScript is the "if" statement.
```

- The "if" Statement:

The "if" statement executes a block of code if a given condition is true.

```javascript
var age = 25;

if (age >= 18) {
  console.log("You are an adult.");
} else {
  console.log("You are a minor.");
}
```

- The "else if" Statement:

The "else if" statement allows you to specify multiple conditions to be checked.

```javascript
var grade = 80;

if (grade >= 90) {
  console.log("Excellent!");
} else if (grade >= 80) {
```

```javascript
  console.log("Good job!");
} else if (grade >= 70) {
  console.log("Keep it up!");
} else {
  console.log("You can do better!");
}
```

- The "switch" Statement:

The "switch" statement provides an alternative way to handle multiple conditions.

```javascript
var day = "Monday";

switch (day) {
  case "Monday":
    console.log("It's the start of the week.");
    break;
  case "Tuesday":
  case "Wednesday":
  case "Thursday":
    console.log("It's a weekday.");
    break;
```

```
   case "Friday":
     console.log("It's finally Friday!");
     break;
   default:
     console.log("It's the weekend!");
}
```

2. Loops:

Loops allow you to execute a block of code repeatedly until a certain condition is met. There are three types of loops in JavaScript: "for" loop, "while" loop, and "do-while" loop.

- The "for" Loop:

The "for" loop is commonly used when you know the exact number of iterations.

```javascript
for (var i = 0; i < 5; i++) {
  console.log("Iteration number: " + i);
}
```

- The "while" Loop:

The "while" loop continues executing a block of code as long as the specified condition is true.

```javascript
var count = 0;

while (count < 5) {
  console.log("Count: " + count);
  count++;
}
```

- The "do-while" Loop:

The "do-while" loop is similar to the "while" loop, but it always executes the code block at least once before checking the condition.

```javascript
var x = 1;

do {
  console.log("Value of x: " + x);
  x++;
} while (x <= 5);
```

3. Loop Control Statements:

Loop control statements allow you to modify the behavior of loops.

- The "break" Statement:

The "break" statement terminates the loop prematurely.

```javascript
for (var i = 0; i < 10; i++) {
  if (i === 5) {
    break;
  }
  console.log(i);
}
```

- The "continue" Statement:

The "continue" statement skips the current iteration and proceeds to the next iteration.

```javascript
for (var i = 0; i < 10; i++) {
  if (i === 5) {
```

```
    continue;

  }

  console.log(i);

}
```
```

In conclusion, conditional statements and loops are essential constructs in JavaScript for controlling the flow of your code and performing repetitive tasks. Understanding how to use these features effectively will enable you to build more sophisticated and dynamic applications. Practice implementing different conditional statements and loops in your JavaScript projects to improve your programming skills. Happy coding!

## 3.6. Functions in JavaScript

Functions are a core concept in JavaScript, allowing you to encapsulate reusable blocks of code and execute them whenever needed. They play a crucial role in organizing and structuring your code, making it more modular and maintainable. In this section, we will explore the basics of functions in JavaScript, including how to define functions, pass arguments, return values, and use anonymous functions.

**1. Defining Functions:**

In JavaScript, you can define functions using the "function" keyword, followed by the function name, a list of parameters (if any), and the function body enclosed in curly braces.

```javascript
function greet(name) {

  console.log("Hello, " + name + "!");
```
```

```
}
```

2. Function Invocation:

To execute a function, you simply need to call it by its name, followed by parentheses, and provide any required arguments.

```javascript
greet("Alice"); // Output: Hello, Alice!
```

3. Function Parameters and Arguments:

Parameters are variables defined in the function's declaration, while arguments are the actual values passed into the function when it is called.

```javascript
function add(a, b) {
  return a + b;
}

var result = add(5, 3);
console.log(result); // Output: 8
```

4. Return Statement:

Functions can return values using the "return" statement. When the function is called, the "return" statement will immediately terminate the function and pass the specified value back to the caller.

```javascript
function multiply(a, b) {
  return a * b;
}

var product = multiply(2, 4);
console.log(product); // Output: 8
```

5. Anonymous Functions:

Anonymous functions, also known as function expressions, are functions without a name. They are often used as callbacks or assigned to variables.

```javascript
var greet = function (name) {
  console.log("Hello, " + name + "!");
};
```

```javascript
greet("Bob"); // Output: Hello, Bob!
```

6. Higher-Order Functions:

In JavaScript, functions can also be passed as arguments to other functions or returned from functions. Functions that operate on other functions are known as higher-order functions.

```javascript
function operate(operation, a, b) {
  return operation(a, b);
}

function add(a, b) {
  return a + b;
}

function subtract(a, b) {
  return a - b;
}

console.log(operate(add, 3, 2));     // Output: 5
console.log(operate(subtract, 6, 3)); // Output: 3
```

7. Function Scope:

JavaScript has function scope, which means variables declared within a function are only accessible within that function.

```javascript
function example() {
  var x = 10;
  console.log(x);
}

example(); // Output: 10

console.log(x); // Throws an error - x is not defined
```

8. Arrow Functions:

Arrow functions provide a concise syntax for writing functions, especially when the function body consists of a single statement.

```javascript
var multiply = (a, b) => a * b;

console.log(multiply(3, 4)); // Output: 12
```

In conclusion, functions are a fundamental building block in JavaScript, enabling you to create reusable and modular code. Understanding how to define, invoke, and use functions effectively will greatly enhance your JavaScript programming skills. Practice creating various types of functions, including anonymous functions and arrow functions, to become more proficient in JavaScript development. Happy coding!

3.7. DOM Manipulation: Interacting with Web Pages

The Document Object Model (DOM) is a critical part of web development, providing a structured representation of HTML documents. With JavaScript, you can dynamically manipulate the DOM, allowing you to change the content, structure, and style of web pages. In this section, we will explore DOM manipulation techniques, including selecting elements, modifying content, adding and removing elements, and handling events.

1. Accessing DOM Elements:

To interact with elements in the DOM, you first need to select them. JavaScript provides various methods to access DOM elements based on their tags, IDs, classes, or other attributes.

```javascript
// Accessing elements by ID

const header = document.getElementById("header");


// Accessing elements by tag name

const paragraphs = document.getElementsByTagName("p");
```

```javascript
// Accessing elements by class name
const buttons = document.getElementsByClassName("btn");


// Accessing elements by query selector
const title = document.querySelector("#title");
const firstButton = document.querySelector(".btn");
```

2. Modifying Element Content:

Once you have selected an element, you can change its content, such as text or HTML, using properties like `innerHTML`, `textContent`, or `innerText`.

```javascript
const title = document.getElementById("title");


// Changing text content
title.textContent = "Hello, JavaScript!";


// Changing HTML content
title.innerHTML = "<em>Hello, JavaScript!</em>";
```

3. Adding and Removing Elements:

JavaScript enables you to add new elements to the DOM or remove existing ones dynamically.

```javascript
const container = document.getElementById("container");

// Creating a new element
const newParagraph = document.createElement("p");
newParagraph.textContent = "This is a new paragraph.";

// Appending the new element to the container
container.appendChild(newParagraph);

// Removing an existing element
const oldElement = document.getElementById("old-element");
container.removeChild(oldElement);
```

4. Modifying Element Attributes and Styles:

You can also change element attributes, such as `src`, `href`, or `class`, and modify their styles using JavaScript.

```javascript
const image = document.getElementById("image");
```

```javascript
// Changing the image source
image.src = "new-image.jpg";

// Adding a new CSS class to the element
image.classList.add("bordered");

// Changing the element's style
image.style.border = "1px solid red";
```

5. Handling Events:

Event handling is crucial for creating interactive web pages. You can use JavaScript to listen for various events, such as clicks, keypresses, or form submissions, and execute corresponding functions when events occur.

```javascript
const button = document.getElementById("button");

// Adding an event listener for the click event
button.addEventListener("click", function() {
  console.log("Button clicked!");
});
```

6. Event Propagation:

DOM events follow a capturing and bubbling phase. By default, events bubble up from the target element to its parent elements. You can stop event propagation using the `stopPropagation()` method.

```javascript
const container = document.getElementById("container");

container.addEventListener("click", function(event) {
  console.log("Container clicked!");
  event.stopPropagation(); // Stop event from bubbling up to other elements
});
```

7. Handling Form Submissions:

JavaScript can be used to handle form submissions, validate input, and prevent the default form submission behavior.

```html
<form id="myForm">
  <input type="text" id="username" required>
  <input type="submit" value="Submit">
</form>
```

```javascript
const form = document.getElementById("myForm");

form.addEventListener("submit", function(event) {
  event.preventDefault(); // Prevent the form from submitting

  const username = document.getElementById("username").value;
  console.log("Username submitted: " + username);
});
```

In conclusion, DOM manipulation is a powerful capability of JavaScript, allowing you to create dynamic and interactive web pages. Understanding how to access, modify, and handle elements in the DOM is essential for modern web development. Practice using DOM manipulation techniques to build engaging web applications and enhance user experiences. Happy coding!

3.8. Introduction to Asynchronous Programming with Promises

Asynchronous programming is a crucial aspect of modern web development, allowing JavaScript to handle time-consuming operations without blocking the execution of other code. Traditionally, callbacks were used to handle asynchronous operations, but they could lead to callback hell and make code difficult to read and maintain. To address these issues, ECMAScript 6 (ES6) introduced Promises, a powerful mechanism to handle asynchronous tasks in a more organized and readable way.

1. Understanding Asynchronous Operations:

Asynchronous operations are tasks that do not occur immediately but require some time to complete, such as reading data from a server, fetching API data, or performing file I/O. In JavaScript, these operations are typically performed using functions like `setTimeout`, `fetch`, or `XMLHttpRequest`.

```javascript
// Asynchronous function using setTimeout
console.log("Start");
setTimeout(function() {
  console.log("Timeout done");
}, 2000);
console.log("End");
```

Output:
```
Start
End
Timeout done
```

2. Callbacks and Callback Hell:

Before Promises, callbacks were commonly used to handle asynchronous tasks. However, chaining multiple callbacks could lead to callback hell, where code becomes nested and hard to manage.

```javascript
function fetchData(callback) {
  // Simulating asynchronous data fetching
  setTimeout(function() {
    const data = { name: "John", age: 30 };
    callback(data);
  }, 1000);
}


fetchData(function(userData) {
  console.log("User data:", userData);
  fetchData(function(userPosts) {
    console.log("User posts:", userPosts);
    fetchData(function(userPhotos) {
      console.log("User photos:", userPhotos);
    });
  });
});
```

3. Introduction to Promises:

Promises provide an elegant solution to the callback hell problem. A Promise is an object that represents a future value or an error that will be resolved asynchronously. It has three states:

pending, fulfilled, or rejected. Promises simplify asynchronous code and allow easier error handling.

```javascript
function fetchData() {
  return new Promise(function(resolve, reject) {
    // Simulating asynchronous data fetching
    setTimeout(function() {
      const data = { name: "John", age: 30 };
      resolve(data);
    }, 1000);
  });
}

fetchData()
  .then(function(userData) {
    console.log("User data:", userData);
    return fetchData();
  })
  .then(function(userPosts) {
    console.log("User posts:", userPosts);
    return fetchData();
  })
  .then(function(userPhotos) {
    console.log("User photos:", userPhotos);
```

```
})
.catch(function(error) {
  console.error("Error:", error);
});
```
```

## 4. Chaining Promises:

Promises support chaining, which allows you to write cleaner and more structured code. Each `.then` block returns a new Promise, enabling you to perform sequential operations.

## 5. Handling Errors with Promises:

Using the `.catch` method, you can handle errors that occur during the Promise chain. If any Promise in the chain rejects, the control flows to the nearest `.catch` block.

```javascript
function fetchData() {
  return new Promise(function(resolve, reject) {
    // Simulating asynchronous data fetching
    setTimeout(function() {
      const data = { name: "John", age: 30 };
      // Simulating an error
      // reject("Data not available");
      resolve(data);
```
```

```javascript
  }, 1000);
 });
}


fetchData()
 .then(function(userData) {
  console.log("User data:", userData);
  return fetchData();
 })
 .then(function(userPosts) {
  console.log("User posts:", userPosts);
  return fetchData();
 })
 .then(function(userPhotos) {
  console.log("User photos:", userPhotos);
 })
 .catch(function(error) {
  console.error("Error:", error);
 });
```
```

## 6. Promise.all and Promise.race:

Promise.all allows you to execute multiple Promises simultaneously and wait for all of them to resolve before proceeding.
```

```javascript
const promise1 = fetchData();

const promise2 = fetchData();

const promise3 = fetchData();


Promise.all([promise1, promise2, promise3])

  .then(function(data) {

   console.log("All data:", data);

  })

  .catch(function(error) {

   console.error("Error:", error);

  });
```

Promise.race, on the other hand, resolves or rejects as soon as any of the Promises in the array is resolved or rejected.

```javascript
const promise1 = fetchData();

const promise2 = fetchData();


Promise.race([promise1, promise2])

  .then(function(data) {

   console.log("First resolved data:", data);
```

```
})
.catch(function(error) {
  console.error("Error:", error);
});
```
```

In conclusion, Promises are a powerful tool to manage asynchronous tasks in JavaScript. They simplify the handling of asynchronous code, making it more readable and maintainable. Understanding Promises is crucial for modern web development, as many APIs and libraries now use Promises for handling asynchronous operations. Practice using Promises to perform asynchronous tasks effectively and create responsive web applications. Happy coding!
```

CHAPTER IV
Exploring Ruby

4.1 Installing Ruby and Development Environment Setup

Ruby is a dynamic, object-oriented programming language known for its simplicity and productivity. In this chapter, we will guide you through the process of installing Ruby on your system and setting up a development environment, enabling you to start coding with Ruby.

1. Installing Ruby:

Before you begin, ensure you have administrative privileges on your computer, as the installation process may require certain permissions.

For Windows Users:

1. Visit the official Ruby website (https://www.ruby-lang.org/en/downloads/) and download the latest Ruby installer for Windows.

2. Run the downloaded installer and follow the on-screen instructions to complete the installation.

3. After installation, open the command prompt and type `ruby -v` to check if Ruby is installed correctly. It should display the installed Ruby version.

For macOS Users:

1. Ruby is pre-installed on macOS. Open the Terminal and type `ruby -v` to check the installed Ruby version.

For Linux Users:

1. Open the Terminal and type the following command to install Ruby using the package manager specific to your Linux distribution:

   - Debian/Ubuntu: `sudo apt-get install ruby-full`

   - Fedora: `sudo dnf install ruby`

   - CentOS/RHEL: `sudo yum install ruby`

2. After installation, type `ruby -v` to check if Ruby is installed correctly.

2. Setting Up a Text Editor:

To write Ruby code, you need a text editor. There are many options available, and you can choose the one that best suits your preferences. Some popular text editors for Ruby development include:

- Visual Studio Code (VSCode)

- Sublime Text

- Atom

- RubyMine (specialized Ruby IDE)

Download and install the text editor of your choice, and you'll be ready to start coding in Ruby.

3. Interactive Ruby (IRB):

Ruby comes with an interactive shell called IRB, which stands for Interactive Ruby. It allows you to run Ruby code interactively, which is excellent for testing snippets of code or exploring language features.

To use IRB:

1. Open the command prompt or terminal.

2. Type `irb` and press Enter. This will launch the IRB shell.

3. Now you can enter Ruby expressions and see their results immediately. For example:

```
irb(main):001:0> 5 + 3
=> 8
irb(main):002:0> "Hello, " + "Ruby"
=> "Hello, Ruby"
```

To exit IRB, type `exit`.

4. Writing Your First Ruby Program:

Let's start by writing a simple "Hello, World!" program in Ruby:

1. Open your text editor and create a new file named `hello.rb`.

2. Add the following code to the `hello.rb` file:

```ruby
puts "Hello, World!"
```

3. Save the file.

4. Open the command prompt or terminal and navigate to the directory where you saved the `hello.rb` file.

5. Type `ruby hello.rb` and press Enter.

You should see the output:

```
Hello, World!
```

Congratulations! You have written and executed your first Ruby program.

5. Installing RubyGems:

RubyGems is a package manager for Ruby libraries, also known as "gems." It allows you to easily install, manage, and use Ruby libraries in your projects.

RubyGems usually comes pre-installed with Ruby. To check if you have RubyGems installed, type `gem -v` in the command prompt or terminal.

If you don't have RubyGems installed or need to update it, follow these steps:

1. Open the command prompt or terminal.

2. Type `gem update --system` and press Enter. This will update RubyGems to the latest version.

3. After the update is complete, type `gem -v` to verify the installation.

Conclusion:

With Ruby successfully installed and your development environment set up, you are now ready to embark on your Ruby journey. This chapter has laid the foundation for your exploration of Ruby programming. In the following chapters, we will dive deeper into the language's features, data structures, and advanced concepts to sharpen your Ruby skills.

Happy coding!

4.2. Understanding Ruby's Data Types and Variables

In Ruby, data types and variables play a crucial role in storing and manipulating data. Understanding them is fundamental to becoming proficient in Ruby programming. In this section, we will explore the various data types available in Ruby and how to work with variables to store and retrieve data.

1. Data Types in Ruby:

Ruby is a dynamically-typed language, which means you don't need to declare the data type of a variable explicitly. The data type is determined at runtime based on the value assigned to the variable. Ruby supports the following basic data types:

1.1. Integers:

Integers are whole numbers without a decimal point. They can be positive, negative, or zero. Ruby automatically allocates the appropriate amount of memory for integers based on the platform.

Example:

```ruby
age = 25
```

1.2. Floats:

Floats represent numbers with a decimal point. They are used for storing floating-point or real numbers.

Example:

```ruby
price = 49.99
```

1.3. Strings:

Strings represent sequences of characters enclosed in single or double quotes. Ruby treats single quotes and double quotes differently, where double quotes allow for string interpolation.

Example:

```ruby
name = "John Doe"
```

1.4. Booleans:

Booleans represent the logical values of true or false. They are commonly used in conditional statements and control flow.

Example:

```ruby
is_raining = true
```

1.5. Arrays:

Arrays are ordered collections of elements. They can store multiple values of any data type, and each element in the array is accessed using an index starting from 0.

Example:

```ruby
numbers = [1, 2, 3, 4, 5]
```

1.6. Hashes:

Hashes, also known as dictionaries or associative arrays in other languages, are collections of key-value pairs. Each key in the hash must be unique, and the value can be of any data type.

Example:

```ruby
person = { "name" => "Alice", "age" => 30, "email" => "alice@example.com" }
```

```

### 1.7. Symbols:

Symbols are lightweight identifiers represented by a colon followed by the symbol's name. They are immutable and unique, making them ideal for use as keys in hashes.

Example:

```ruby
status = :success
```

1.8. Nil:

Nil represents the absence of a value. It is similar to null in other programming languages.

Example:

```ruby
result = nil
```

2. Variables in Ruby:
```

Variables are used to store data of various data types, and they are identified by their names. In Ruby, variables start with a lowercase letter or an underscore (_) followed by letters, digits, or underscores.

2.1. Assigning Values to Variables:

To assign a value to a variable, you use the assignment operator (=). The value on the right side of the operator is assigned to the variable on the left side.

Example:

```ruby
age = 25
name = "John Doe"
```

2.2. Variable Naming Conventions:

To write clean and readable code, follow these naming conventions for variables:

- Use descriptive names that indicate the variable's purpose.
- Use snake_case for variable names (e.g., user_age, first_name).
- Avoid using reserved keywords as variable names (e.g., if, else, class).

2.3. Variable Scope:

Ruby has three types of variable scope:

- Local variables: Defined within a method or block and are accessible only within that context.

- Instance variables: Prefixed with @ and are accessible across different methods within the same object instance.

- Global variables: Prefixed with $ and are accessible throughout the entire Ruby program.

Example:

```ruby
def greet
  name = "Alice"    # Local variable
  @age = 30         # Instance variable
  $count = 0        # Global variable
end
```

2.4. Constants:

Constants are variables that hold values that should not be changed throughout the program's execution. They start with an uppercase letter and should be used for values that remain constant.

Example:

```ruby
```

```
PI = 3.14159
```

3. Type Conversion (Casting):

In Ruby, you can convert one data type to another using type conversion methods or casting.

3.1. To Integer (to_i):

```ruby
number_as_string = "10"
number = number_as_string.to_i   # Result: 10
```

3.2. To Float (to_f):

```ruby
number_as_string = "10.5"
number = number_as_string.to_f   # Result: 10.5
```

3.3. To String (to_s):

```ruby
```

```
number = 10
number_as_string = number


.to_s   # Result: "10"
```

Conclusion:

Understanding data types and variables is essential in any programming language, and Ruby is no exception. In this chapter, we explored the various data types available in Ruby and how to work with variables to store and retrieve data. By mastering these concepts, you are equipped with the foundation needed to build more sophisticated Ruby programs in the upcoming chapters. Happy coding!

4.3. Working with Arrays and Hashes

Arrays and Hashes are fundamental data structures in Ruby that allow you to organize and manipulate collections of data efficiently. In this section, we will dive deeper into working with arrays and hashes, understanding their properties, and exploring various methods to interact with them.

1. Working with Arrays:

1.1. Creating Arrays:

To create an array in Ruby, you can use square brackets [] and separate the elements with commas. Arrays can store elements of different data types, and they are ordered and indexed starting from 0.

Example:

```ruby
numbers = [1, 2, 3, 4, 5]
fruits = ["apple", "banana", "orange"]
```

1.2. Accessing Array Elements:

You can access individual elements in an array using their index. Indexing starts at 0 for the first element, 1 for the second, and so on.

Example:

```ruby
puts numbers[0]    # Output: 1
puts fruits[1]     # Output: "banana"
```

1.3. Array Methods:

Ruby provides a wide range of built-in methods to work with arrays. Some commonly used methods include:

- `length` or `size`: Returns the number of elements in the array.

- `push` or `<<`: Appends an element to the end of the array.

- `pop`: Removes and returns the last element of the array.

- `include?`: Checks if an element exists in the array.

- `sort`: Sorts the array elements in ascending order.

Example:

```ruby
puts numbers.length        # Output: 5
fruits.push("grape")       # ["apple", "banana", "orange", "grape"]
last_fruit = fruits.pop     # last_fruit = "grape", fruits = ["apple", "banana", "orange"]
puts fruits.include?("apple")  # Output: true
puts numbers.sort          # Output: [1, 2, 3, 4, 5]
```

1.4. Iterating Over Arrays:

You can use loops or iterators to traverse elements in an array. Common iterators like `each`, `map`, and `select` simplify array manipulation.

Example:

```ruby
fruits.each do |fruit|
```

```
  puts "I love #{fruit}s"
end


numbers_squared = numbers.map do |num|
  num * num
end


even_numbers = numbers.select do |num|
  num.even?
end
```

2. Working with Hashes:

2.1. Creating Hashes:

Hashes in Ruby consist of key-value pairs. To create a hash, you use curly braces {} and separate each pair with a comma. Accessing elements in a hash is done using their keys.

Example:


```ruby
person = { "name" => "Alice", "age" => 30, "email" => "alice@example.com" }
```

2.2. Accessing Hash Elements:

To access the value of a specific key in a hash, you use square brackets [] with the key as the index.

Example:

```ruby
puts person["name"]      # Output: "Alice"
puts person["age"]      # Output: 30
```

2.3. Hash Methods:

Ruby provides several methods to interact with hashes. Some common methods include:

- `keys`: Returns an array of all the keys in the hash.

- `values`: Returns an array of all the values in the hash.

- `has_key?` or `key?`: Checks if a specific key exists in the hash.

- `delete`: Removes a key-value pair from the hash.

Example:

```ruby
puts person.keys      # Output: ["name", "age", "email"]
```

```
puts person.values       # Output: ["Alice", 30, "alice@example.com"]

puts person.has_key?("name")   # Output: true

person.delete("email")    # person = { "name" => "Alice", "age" => 30 }
```

2.4. Iterating Over Hashes:

You can use iterators like `each` to iterate over key-value pairs in a hash.

Example:

```ruby
person.each do |key, value|
  puts "#{key}: #{value}"
end
```

Conclusion:

In this chapter, we explored working with arrays and hashes in Ruby. Arrays are versatile data structures used to store lists of elements, while hashes allow you to organize data using key-value pairs. Understanding how to create, access, and manipulate arrays and hashes is crucial for effective data management in Ruby. With these skills, you can confidently work with collections of data and perform various operations on them as you progress in your Ruby journey. Happy coding!

4.4. Control Structures: Conditionals and Loops

Control structures, such as conditionals and loops, are essential components of any programming language. They allow you to control the flow of your code, execute specific blocks of code based on certain conditions, and repeat code execution until a certain condition is met. In this section, we will explore conditional statements and different types of loops available in Ruby.

1. Conditional Statements:

Conditional statements in Ruby allow you to make decisions and execute different blocks of code based on specific conditions. The most commonly used conditional statement is the `if` statement.

1.1. The `if` Statement:

The `if` statement executes a block of code only if a given condition is true.

Syntax:

```ruby
if condition
  # Code block executed if the condition is true
end
```

Example:

```ruby
age = 18
if age >= 18
  puts "You are an adult."
end
```

1.2. The `if-else` Statement:

The `if-else` statement allows you to execute one block of code if the condition is true and another block if the condition is false.

Syntax:

```ruby
if condition
  # Code block executed if the condition is true
else
  # Code block executed if the condition is false
end
```

Example:

```ruby
```

```ruby
age = 16
if age >= 18
  puts "You are an adult."
else
  puts "You are a minor."
end
```

1.3. The `if-elsif-else` Statement:

The `if-elsif-else` statement enables you to check multiple conditions and execute different code blocks based on the first condition that evaluates to true.

Syntax:

```ruby
if condition1
  # Code block executed if condition1 is true
elsif condition2
  # Code block executed if condition2 is true
else
  # Code block executed if all conditions are false
end
```

Example:

```ruby
grade = 85
if grade >= 90
  puts "A"
elsif grade >= 80
  puts "B"
elsif grade >= 70
  puts "C"
else
  puts "D"
end
```

1.4. The `unless` Statement:

The `unless` statement is the opposite of the `if` statement. It executes a block of code only if the condition is false.

Syntax:

```ruby
unless condition
  # Code block executed if the condition is false
```

```
end
```

Example:

```ruby
temperature = 25
unless temperature > 30
  puts "It's not too hot today."
end
```

2. Loops:

Loops in Ruby allow you to repeat code execution multiple times. There are different types of loops available, such as `while`, `until`, `for`, and `each`.

2.1. The `while` Loop:

The `while` loop repeats a block of code while a certain condition is true.

Syntax:

```ruby
while condition
```

```
  # Code block executed while the condition is true
end
```

Example:

```ruby
count = 1
while count <= 5
  puts "Count: #{count}"
  count += 1
end
```

2.2. The `until` Loop:

The `until` loop repeats a block of code until a certain condition is true.

Syntax:

```ruby
until condition
  # Code block executed until the condition is true
end
```

```
```

Example:

```ruby
count = 1
until count > 5
  puts "Count: #{count}"
  count += 1
end
```

2.3. The `for` Loop:

The `for` loop allows you to iterate over a range of values or elements in an array.

Syntax:

```ruby
for variable in range or array
  # Code block executed for each value in the range or element in the array
end
```

Example:

```ruby
for i in 1..5
  puts "Number: #{i}"
end

fruits = ["apple", "banana", "orange"]
for fruit in fruits
  puts "I love #{fruit}s"
end
```

2.4. The `each` Loop:

The `each` loop is another way to iterate over elements in an array.

Syntax:

```ruby
array.each do |variable|
  # Code block executed for each element in the array
end
```

Example:

```ruby
numbers = [1, 2, 3, 4, 5]
numbers.each do |num|
  puts num * 2
end
```

Conclusion:

In this chapter, we explored control structures in Ruby, including conditional statements and loops. These features are essential for making decisions and repeating code execution, allowing you to create powerful and dynamic programs. By mastering conditional statements and various types of loops, you can efficiently control the flow of your Ruby code and build robust applications that meet specific requirements. Happy coding!

4.5. Methods and Functions in Ruby

Methods and functions are fundamental building blocks in any programming language, including Ruby. They enable you to break down complex tasks into smaller, reusable pieces of code. In this section, we will delve into methods and functions in Ruby, how to define them, pass arguments, and return values.

1. Understanding Methods in Ruby:

In Ruby, a method is a block of code that performs a specific action and can be called multiple times throughout the program. Methods are defined within classes, and they encapsulate behavior that can be used by objects of that class.

1.1. Defining a Method:

To define a method in Ruby, you use the `def` keyword, followed by the method name and any parameters it takes (if any). The method body is then enclosed within a set of curly braces or an `end` keyword.

Syntax:

```ruby
def method_name(parameter1, parameter2)
  # method body
end
```

Example:

```ruby
def greet(name)
  puts "Hello, #{name}!"
end
```

1.2. Calling a Method:

After defining a method, you can call it by using its name followed by any necessary arguments in parentheses.

Example:

```ruby
greet("Alice")
```

This will output: `Hello, Alice!`

1.3. Default Parameters:

You can assign default values to parameters in a method. If a value is not provided for that parameter when the method is called, it will use the default value instead.

Example:

```ruby
def greet(name = "Guest")
  puts "Hello, #{name}!"
end
```

1.4. Returning Values:

Methods can also return values. In Ruby, the last evaluated expression in a method is automatically returned as the result.

Example:

```ruby
def add(a, b)
  a + b
end

result = add(3, 5)
puts result
```

This will output: `8`

2. Functions in Ruby:

Ruby does not have a built-in function concept like some other languages, but you can use methods to achieve the same functionality.

3. Built-in Ruby Methods:

Ruby comes with a rich set of built-in methods that are part of the core classes. For example, strings and arrays have many useful methods that you can use directly without defining them yourself.

Example:

```ruby
# Using built-in string methods
name = "John Doe"
puts name.upcase
puts name.length

# Using built-in array methods
numbers = [1, 2, 3, 4, 5]
puts numbers.sum
puts numbers.reverse
```

4. Recursion:

Recursion is a technique where a method calls itself to solve a problem. It is essential to understand recursion to tackle complex algorithms and data structures.

Example:

```ruby
def factorial(n)
 if n == 0 || n == 1
  return 1
 else
  return n * factorial(n - 1)
 end
end


puts factorial(5)
```


This will output: `120`

5. Conclusion:

In this chapter, we explored methods and functions in Ruby, how to define them, pass arguments, and return values. By using methods effectively, you can create more organized and modular code, making your Ruby programs easier to read, maintain, and debug. Understanding built-in Ruby methods and recursion will also empower you to solve complex problems efficiently. Keep practicing and honing your Ruby skills, and you'll become a proficient Ruby programmer in no time!

4.6. Classes and Objects: Object-Oriented Programming in Ruby

Object-Oriented Programming (OOP) is a powerful paradigm widely used in modern programming languages, including Ruby. It allows you to model real-world entities and their interactions as objects. In this section, we will delve into classes and objects in Ruby, how to define them, create instances, and work with their attributes and methods.

1. Understanding Classes and Objects in Ruby:

In Ruby, a class is a blueprint for creating objects. It defines the attributes and behaviors that objects of that class will have. Objects are instances of classes, and they represent individual entities with unique data.

1.1. Defining a Class:

To define a class in Ruby, you use the `class` keyword, followed by the class name (by convention, class names start with an uppercase letter). Inside the class, you can define attributes using instance variables (`@variable_name`) and methods.

Syntax:

```ruby
class ClassName
  # attributes and methods
end
```

Example:

```ruby
```

```ruby
class Dog
  def initialize(name, breed)
    @name = name
    @breed = breed
  end

  def bark
    puts "Woof! Woof!"
  end
end
```

1.2. Creating Objects (Instances):

To create an object (an instance of a class) in Ruby, you call the `new` method on the class and pass any required arguments to the `initialize` method.

Example:

```ruby
dog1 = Dog.new("Buddy", "Golden Retriever")
dog2 = Dog.new("Max", "Labrador")
```

1.3. Accessing Attributes:

Instance variables in a class can be accessed using getter and setter methods. Ruby provides the `attr_reader`, `attr_writer`, and `attr_accessor` methods for this purpose.

Example:

```ruby
class Dog
  attr_reader :name, :breed
  attr_writer :name
  attr_accessor :age

  def initialize(name, breed)
    @name = name
    @breed = breed
    @age = 1
  end
end

dog = Dog.new("Buddy", "Golden Retriever")
puts dog.name
dog.name = "Charlie"
puts dog.name
puts dog.age
dog.age = 2
```

```
puts dog.age
```

1.4. Class Methods:

A class method is a method that belongs to the class itself, not to individual instances of the class. You define class methods using the `self` keyword.

Example:

```ruby
class Dog
  def self.bark_class_method
    puts "Class Method: Woof! Woof!"
  end
end

Dog.bark_class_method
```

1.5. Inheritance:

Inheritance allows a class to inherit attributes and methods from another class, creating a parent-child relationship. The child class (subclass) inherits all the properties of the parent class (superclass) and can also have its own unique attributes and methods.

Example:

```ruby
class Animal
  def breathe
    puts "Breathing..."
  end
end

class Dog < Animal
  def bark
    puts "Woof! Woof!"
  end
end

dog = Dog.new
dog.breathe
dog.bark
```

2. Conclusion:

In this chapter, we explored classes and objects in Ruby and how to define classes, create instances, and work with their attributes and methods. Object-Oriented Programming is a powerful paradigm that enables you to write modular, reusable, and maintainable code. By mastering classes, objects, and inheritance, you can design elegant and efficient Ruby programs.

Practice building classes and interacting with objects to gain a deeper understanding of OOP concepts in Ruby. With these skills, you'll be well-equipped to develop sophisticated and feature-rich Ruby applications.

4.7. Gems and Libraries: Extending Ruby's Functionality

Ruby is known for its vast collection of gems and libraries, which are packages of pre-written code that extend the language's functionality. These gems and libraries are contributed by the Ruby community and can save you time and effort in building various functionalities in your Ruby projects. In this section, we will explore how to work with gems and libraries, including installation, usage, and some popular examples.

1. Understanding Gems and Libraries in Ruby:

1.1. What are Gems?

Gems are self-contained packages of code that provide specific functionality and can be easily integrated into your Ruby projects. They are distributed through the RubyGems package manager, which is included with Ruby by default. RubyGems allows you to easily install, manage, and remove gems from your development environment.

1.2. Finding and Installing Gems:

To find gems that suit your needs, you can use the RubyGems website (https://rubygems.org/) or the command-line interface. To install a gem, open your terminal or command prompt and use the `gem install` command followed by the gem's name.

Example:

```
gem install nokogiri
```

1.3. Using Gems in Your Code:

Once a gem is installed, you can include it in your Ruby code using the `require` keyword. This loads the gem into your project, making its functionality available for use.

Example:

```ruby
require 'nokogiri'
# Your code that uses Nokogiri goes here
```

1.4. Popular Gems:

There are numerous gems available for various purposes in Ruby. Here are some popular gems with their use cases:

- **Rails:** A powerful web application framework for building web applications quickly and efficiently.

- **RSpec:** A testing framework that allows you to write automated tests for your Ruby code.

- **Devise:** A flexible authentication solution for Rails applications, providing user registration, login, and more.

- **Capybara:** A tool for writing acceptance tests for web applications, simulating user interaction in a browser.

- **Sidekiq:** A background processing library for Rails that allows you to perform asynchronous tasks.

2. Working with Ruby Libraries:

2.1. What are Libraries?

In addition to gems, Ruby also has built-in libraries that come bundled with the language. These libraries provide additional functionality and are part of the standard Ruby distribution. They cover a wide range of tasks, such as file handling, regular expressions, and networking.

2.2. Using Ruby Libraries:

To use a built-in library, you don't need to install anything; it's already available for you. You can include it in your Ruby code using the `require` keyword, just like with gems.

Example:

```ruby
require 'json'
# Your code that uses JSON library goes here
```

2.3. Popular Ruby Libraries:

Ruby comes with a rich set of built-in libraries. Some popular ones include:

- **JSON:** For working with JSON data, including parsing and generating JSON strings.

- **CSV:** For reading and writing Comma-Separated Values (CSV) files.

- **Net::HTTP:** For making HTTP requests, allowing your Ruby programs to interact with web services.

- **Time:** For working with dates and times in Ruby.

- **File:** For basic file operations like reading, writing, and deleting files.

3. Managing Gem Dependencies:

When working with multiple gems, you may encounter situations where gems depend on other gems to function correctly. This can lead to gem version conflicts. To manage gem dependencies effectively, you can use a `Gemfile` in your project's root directory.

3.1. Creating a Gemfile:

To create a `Gemfile`, simply create a plain text file named `Gemfile` (with no file extension) in your project's root folder.

Example:

```ruby
# Gemfile
source 'https://rubygems.org'
```

```
gem 'nokogiri'

gem 'rails'

```
```

3.2. Installing Gems from Gemfile:

To install all the gems listed in your `Gemfile`, run the `bundle install` command in your terminal or command prompt.

3.3. Updating Gems:

To update gems to their latest versions, use the `bundle update` command.

4. Conclusion:

Gems and libraries play a crucial role in extending Ruby's capabilities. By leveraging existing code through gems and built-in libraries, you can significantly speed up the development process and focus on building the unique parts of your projects. Be sure to explore the vast collection of gems available in the Ruby community and make use of built-in libraries to handle common programming tasks efficiently. Keep your gem dependencies organized using a `Gemfile` to ensure a smooth development experience. Happy coding!
```

CHAPTER V
Advanced Concepts in Programming

5.1 File Handling: Reading and Writing Data

File handling is an essential aspect of programming that involves reading data from files or writing data to files. It enables programs to interact with external data sources, such as text files, CSV files, or even databases. In this section, we will explore various techniques for reading and writing data to files using Python, as it provides a simple yet powerful way to handle files.

1. Reading Data from Files:

1.1 Opening and Closing Files:

To read data from a file, the first step is to open the file in read mode using the `open()` function. The `open()` function takes two arguments: the name of the file and the mode (e.g., "r" for read, "w" for write, "a" for append, etc.).

Example:

```python
# Open a file in read mode

file = open("data.txt", "r")

# Your code to read data from the file goes here

# Don't forget to close the file
```

```
file.close()
```

1.2 Reading the Entire File:

To read the entire contents of a file, you can use the `read()` method. It returns the content of the file as a single string.

Example:

```python
file = open("data.txt", "r")
content = file.read()
print(content)
file.close()
```

1.3 Reading Line by Line:

If a file is large or you only need to process it line by line, you can use a `for` loop to read each line in the file.

Example:

```python
```

```python
file = open("data.txt", "r")
for line in file:
    print(line.strip())  # Strip removes the newline character at the end of each line
file.close()
```

2. Writing Data to Files:

2.1 Opening Files in Write Mode:

To write data to a file, open the file in write mode ("w") using the `open()` function. If the file does not exist, Python will create it. Be careful when opening a file in write mode, as it will overwrite the existing content.

Example:

```python
# Open a file in write mode
file = open("output.txt", "w")
# Your code to write data to the file goes here
# Don't forget to close the file
file.close()
```

2.2 Writing Data:

To write data to a file, you can use the `write()` method of the file object. It takes a single argument, which is the data you want to write.

Example:

```python
file = open("output.txt", "w")
file.write("Hello, world!\n")
file.write("This is a sample text.")
file.close()
```

2.3 Appending Data to Files:

If you want to add data to an existing file without overwriting its content, you can open the file in append mode ("a") instead of write mode.

Example:

```python
file = open("output.txt", "a")
file.write("\nThis is an appended line.")
file.close()
```

3. Handling File Exceptions:

When working with files, it's essential to handle exceptions that may occur, such as when the file does not exist or when there are issues with file permissions. Using a `try-except` block can help you handle such exceptions gracefully.

Example:

```python
try:
    file = open("data.txt", "r")
    content = file.read()
    print(content)
    file.close()
except FileNotFoundError:
    print("File not found.")
except PermissionError:
    print("Permission denied.")
```

4. Closing Files Automatically with "with" Statement:

To ensure that files are properly closed even if an exception occurs, you can use the `with` statement. It automatically closes the file once the block of code inside it is executed.

Example:

```python
with open("data.txt", "r") as file:
    content = file.read()
    print(content)
```

5. Conclusion:

File handling is a fundamental skill in programming, allowing you to read data from external sources and write data to files for storage or further processing. Python provides simple and efficient ways to work with files, making it easy to manipulate data and perform various file-related operations. Remember to close files after use, handle exceptions gracefully, and consider using the "with" statement for automatic file handling. Happy coding!

5.2. Error Handling: Dealing with Exceptions

Error handling is a crucial aspect of programming to ensure the reliability and robustness of our code. It involves identifying and handling errors or exceptional situations that may occur during the execution of a program. In Python, exceptions are used to handle such errors gracefully. An exception is an object that represents an error or unexpected behavior that disrupts the normal flow of a program.

1. Understanding Exceptions in Python:

In Python, when an error occurs, the program stops execution and raises an exception. The exception contains information about the type of error and the location in the code where the error occurred. By using exception handling, we can catch and handle these exceptions, allowing the program to continue running without crashing.

2. The try-except Block:

The most common way to handle exceptions in Python is by using the `try-except` block. The `try` block contains the code that might raise an exception. If an exception occurs in the `try` block, the code in the corresponding `except` block is executed.

Example:

```python
try:
    x = 10 / 0  # This will raise a ZeroDivisionError
except ZeroDivisionError:
    print("Error: Cannot divide by zero.")
```

3. Handling Multiple Exceptions:

You can handle multiple exceptions using multiple `except` blocks or by using a single `except` block with a tuple of exception types.

Example using multiple `except` blocks:

```python
```

```python
try:
    num = int(input("Enter a number: "))
    result = 10 / num
except ZeroDivisionError:
    print("Error: Cannot divide by zero.")
except ValueError:
    print("Error: Invalid input. Please enter a valid number.")
```

Example using a single `except` block with a tuple:

```python
try:
    num = int(input("Enter a number: "))
    result = 10 / num
except (ZeroDivisionError, ValueError):
    print("Error: Invalid input or cannot divide by zero.")
```

4. The else Clause:

The `else` clause is executed if no exceptions are raised in the `try` block. It is useful when you want to perform some actions only when the code in the `try` block runs successfully.

Example:

```python
try:
    num = int(input("Enter a number: "))
    result = 10 / num
except (ZeroDivisionError, ValueError):
    print("Error: Invalid input or cannot divide by zero.")
else:
    print("The result is:", result)
```

5. The finally Clause:

The `finally` clause is used to define code that will be executed no matter what, whether an exception is raised or not. It is commonly used for cleanup actions, such as closing files or releasing resources.

Example:

```python
try:
    file = open("data.txt", "r")
    # Your code to read data from the file goes here
except FileNotFoundError:
    print("File not found.")
```

finally:

    file.close() # This will be executed regardless of whether an exception occurred or not

```

## 6. Raising Custom Exceptions:

In addition to handling built-in exceptions, you can also raise custom exceptions to handle specific situations in your code.

Example:

```python
def divide(x, y):
    if y == 0:
        raise ValueError("Cannot divide by zero.")
    return x / y


try:
    result = divide(10, 0)
except ValueError as e:
    print(e)
```

7. Handling Uncaught Exceptions:
```

If an exception occurs in the program and is not caught by any `try-except` block, Python will print an error message and terminate the program. To prevent this, you can use the `except` block without specifying any exception type to catch all uncaught exceptions.

Example:

```python
try:
    # Your code here
except:
    print("An unexpected error occurred.")
```

8. Conclusion:

Error handling is essential for writing reliable and stable programs. By using the `try-except` block, you can catch and handle exceptions, ensuring that your program continues to run smoothly even when unexpected situations occur. Remember to use specific exception types whenever possible and include appropriate error messages to make debugging easier. Happy coding!

5.3. Regular Expressions: Pattern Matching in Text

Regular expressions, often abbreviated as regex or regexp, are powerful tools used for pattern matching and manipulation in text data. They provide a concise and flexible way to search, extract, and replace specific patterns within strings. Regular expressions are supported in various programming languages, including Python, JavaScript, Ruby, and many others.

1. Introduction to Regular Expressions:

A regular expression is a sequence of characters that forms a search pattern. It can be used to match specific strings or parts of strings based on defined patterns. For example, you can use regular expressions to:

- Validate email addresses, phone numbers, or other patterns in user input.

- Extract specific data from text, such as dates, URLs, or numbers.

- Replace certain patterns with other text.

2. Basic Regular Expression Syntax:

In regular expressions, certain characters have special meanings. For instance:

- `.` (dot): Matches any character except a newline.

- `^` (caret): Matches the beginning of a string.

- `$` (dollar): Matches the end of a string.

- `*` (asterisk): Matches zero or more occurrences of the preceding character.

- `+` (plus): Matches one or more occurrences of the preceding character.

- `?` (question mark): Matches zero or one occurrence of the preceding character.

- `[]` (square brackets): Matches any character within the brackets.

- `|` (pipe): Acts like a logical OR, matches either the expression before or after it.

3. Using Regular Expressions in Python:

Python provides the `re` module for working with regular expressions. The `re` module allows you to compile and use regular expressions for searching and manipulating strings.

Example 1: Matching a Phone Number Pattern

```python
import re

pattern = r"\d{3}-\d{3}-\d{4}"
text = "Call me at 123-456-7890 or 987-654-3210."
matches = re.findall(pattern, text)

print(matches)  # Output: ['123-456-7890', '987-654-3210']
```

Example 2: Extracting Email Addresses

```python
import re

pattern = r"\b[A-Za-z0-9._%+-]+@[A-Za-z0-9.-]+\.[A-Z|a-z]{2,}\b"
text = "Contact us at contact@example.com or info@company.org."
matches = re.findall(pattern, text, re.IGNORECASE)

print(matches)  # Output: ['contact@example.com', 'info@company.org']
```

4. Regular Expression Flags:

In the previous examples, we used the `re.IGNORECASE` flag to make the pattern matching case-insensitive. Regular expression flags modify the behavior of the regular expression. Some common flags include:

- `re.IGNORECASE` (or `re.I`): Makes the pattern matching case-insensitive.

- `re.MULTILINE` (or `re.M`): Allows the pattern to match at the beginning and end of each line.

- `re.DOTALL` (or `re.S`): Allows the dot `.` to match newline characters.

5. Regular Expression Methods:

The `re` module in Python provides various methods for working with regular expressions, such as:

- `re.search(pattern, text)`: Searches for the first occurrence of the pattern in the text.

- `re.match(pattern, text)`: Checks if the pattern matches at the beginning of the text.

- `re.findall(pattern, text)`: Returns all occurrences of the pattern in the text as a list.

- `re.finditer(pattern, text)`: Returns an iterator yielding match objects for all occurrences.

- `re.sub(pattern, replacement, text)`: Replaces occurrences of the pattern with the replacement text.

6. Escape Characters:

Some characters in regular expressions have special meanings and need to be escaped if you want to match them literally. For example, to match a period `.` in text, you need to use `\.` in the regular expression.

7. Advanced Regular Expression Techniques:

Regular expressions support more advanced techniques, such as:

- Grouping and capturing specific parts of a pattern.

- Using quantifiers like `{}` to specify the number of occurrences.

- Lookahead and lookbehind assertions to match based on context.

8. Conclusion:

Regular expressions are a powerful tool for text manipulation, providing a flexible way to find and extract specific patterns in strings. Understanding regular expressions and how to use them can significantly enhance your text processing capabilities in various programming tasks. Experiment with different patterns and explore the documentation of your programming language's regex module for further understanding and mastery. Happy pattern matching!

5.4. Introduction to Functional Programming

Functional programming is a programming paradigm that treats computation as the evaluation of mathematical functions and avoids changing state and mutable data. It emphasizes the use of pure functions that have no side effects and produce the same output for the same input. Functional programming languages, such as Haskell, Lisp, and Scala, are designed to support this paradigm, but many modern programming languages, including Python, JavaScript, and Ruby, also incorporate functional programming features.

1. Key Concepts of Functional Programming:

1.1 Pure Functions:

A pure function is a function that, given the same input, always produces the same output and has no side effects, meaning it does not modify external state or variables. Pure functions are easy to reason about, test, and parallelize, making code more reliable and easier to maintain.

Example of a Pure Function:

```python
def add(a, b):
    return a + b
```

1.2 Immutability:

In functional programming, data is immutable, meaning once created, it cannot be changed. Instead of modifying existing data, functions create new data structures with the desired changes.

Example of Immutability in Python:

```python
# Creating a new list instead of modifying the existing one
original_list = [1, 2, 3]
new_list = original_list + [4]
```

1.3 Higher-Order Functions:

Higher-order functions are functions that can take other functions as arguments or return functions as results. They enable the composition of functions, making code more concise and expressive.

Example of Higher-Order Function in JavaScript:

```javascript
const numbers = [1, 2, 3, 4];
const double = (x) => x * 2;
const doubledNumbers = numbers.map(double);
```

2. Function Composition:

Functional programming encourages function composition, where functions are combined to create more complex functions. This approach allows developers to build complex operations by chaining simple functions together.

Example of Function Composition in Python:

```python
def add(a, b):
    return a + b

def square(x):
    return x ** 2
```

```
# Combining 'add' and 'square' functions
result = square(add(2, 3))
print(result)  # Output: 25
```

3. Recursion:

Functional programming often relies on recursion, where a function calls itself to solve a problem. Recursive algorithms can be elegant and expressive but may require careful handling to avoid infinite loops.

Example of Recursion in Ruby:

```ruby
def factorial(n)
  if n <= 1
    1
  else
    n * factorial(n - 1)
  end
end

puts factorial(5)  # Output: 120
```

4. Closures:

Closures are functions that capture variables from their surrounding environment, allowing those variables to be accessed even after the outer function has finished executing.

Example of Closure in JavaScript:

```javascript
function makeMultiplier(x) {
  return function(y) {
    return x * y;
  };
}

const multiplyByTwo = makeMultiplier(2);
console.log(multiplyByTwo(5));  // Output: 10
```

5. Benefits and Challenges of Functional Programming:

5.1 Benefits:

- Easier debugging and testing due to pure functions and immutability.

- Improved code readability and maintainability through function composition.

- Simplified parallel processing due to lack of side effects.

- Increased reliability and predictability.

5.2 Challenges:

- Learning curve for developers new to the paradigm.

- Performance concerns in some scenarios due to the creation of new data structures instead of modifying existing ones.

- Difficulty in converting existing imperative codebases to a functional style.

6. Conclusion:

Functional programming is a powerful paradigm that can lead to more robust, reliable, and expressive code. Understanding functional concepts and incorporating them into your programming toolkit can improve the quality of your code and lead to more elegant and maintainable solutions. While functional programming may not be the right fit for every situation, being familiar with its principles and techniques can make you a more well-rounded and versatile programmer. As with any programming paradigm, practice and experimentation are key to mastering functional programming concepts and techniques.

5.5. Working with APIs: Data Retrieval from Web Services

As the internet has evolved, web services and APIs (Application Programming Interfaces) have become essential for accessing and sharing data between different applications and platforms. APIs allow developers to retrieve data, interact with external services, and perform various operations over the internet. In this chapter, we will explore how to work with APIs to retrieve data from web services using popular programming languages like Python, JavaScript, and Ruby.

1. What is an API?

An API is a set of rules and protocols that allows different software applications to communicate with each other. It defines the methods and data formats that applications can use to request and exchange information. APIs are commonly used to enable integration between different systems and to access services provided by other applications or platforms.

2. HTTP and RESTful APIs:

HTTP (Hypertext Transfer Protocol) is the foundation of data communication on the internet. Many APIs are built using HTTP as their underlying protocol, and they follow a set of architectural principles known as REST (Representational State Transfer)ful APIs. RESTful APIs use standard HTTP methods like GET, POST, PUT, DELETE to perform operations on resources identified by URLs.

3. Making API Requests:

To interact with APIs, we need to make HTTP requests to the API endpoints. These requests can be made using various libraries and frameworks available in different programming languages. Let's see examples of making API requests in Python, JavaScript, and Ruby.

Example of Making an API Request in Python:

```python
import requests

url = 'https://api.example.com/data'
response = requests.get(url)


if response.status_code == 200:
```

```python
    data = response.json()
    print(data)
else:
    print('Failed to fetch data from the API')
```

Example of Making an API Request in JavaScript (using Fetch API):

```javascript
fetch('https://api.example.com/data')
    .then(response => response.json())
    .then(data => console.log(data))
    .catch(error => console.error('Failed to fetch data from the API', error));
```

Example of Making an API Request in Ruby (using HTTParty gem):

```ruby
require 'httparty'

url = 'https://api.example.com/data'
response = HTTParty.get(url)

if response.success?
```

```
    data = JSON.parse(response.body)

    puts data
else

    puts 'Failed to fetch data from the API'

end
```

4. Authentication and API Keys:

Some APIs require authentication to access their data. API keys or tokens are commonly used for authentication. Developers need to include these keys in their requests to prove their identity and access the API's resources. The process of authentication varies depending on the API provider.

Example of Making an Authenticated API Request in Python:

```python
import requests

api_key = 'your_api_key_here'
url = f'https://api.example.com/data?api_key={api_key}'
response = requests.get(url)

if response.status_code == 200:
    data = response.json()
    print(data)
```

```
else:

    print('Failed to fetch data from the API')
```

5. Parsing API Responses:

API responses are usually returned in a structured format like JSON (JavaScript Object Notation) or XML (Extensible Markup Language). To work with the retrieved data, we need to parse these responses into usable data structures in our programming language.

Example of Parsing API Response in Python:

```python
import requests

url = 'https://api.example.com/data'
response = requests.get(url)

if response.status_code == 200:
    data = response.json()
    for item in data:
        print(item['name'])
else:
    print('Failed to fetch data from the API')
```

6. Rate Limiting and Pagination:

API providers often enforce rate limits to control the number of requests a user can make within a given time frame. Additionally, when an API returns a large number of results, it may paginate the responses to prevent overwhelming the client with a massive amount of data.

Developers need to handle rate limiting and pagination to avoid API restrictions and efficiently retrieve all the required data.

7. Error Handling:

When working with APIs, there is a possibility of encountering errors. Proper error handling is crucial to gracefully handle failures and provide informative messages to users.

8. Conclusion:

Working with APIs opens up a vast world of possibilities for developers to access data and services from various sources. Whether you are building web applications, mobile apps, or data analysis tools, understanding how to work with APIs is an essential skill. In this chapter, we explored the basics of APIs, making requests, authentication, parsing responses, and dealing with common challenges like rate limiting and pagination. By mastering API usage, you can create more dynamic and interconnected applications that leverage the power of the internet and external services.

5.6. Introduction to Data Science and Machine Learning

Data Science and Machine Learning have revolutionized various industries, enabling businesses to extract valuable insights from vast amounts of data and make data-driven decisions. In this chapter, we will delve into the exciting world of data science and machine learning, exploring the core concepts, techniques, and tools used to analyze data and build predictive models.

1. What is Data Science?

Data Science is an interdisciplinary field that combines techniques from statistics, computer science, and domain knowledge to extract meaningful patterns and insights from raw data. The data science process involves collecting, cleaning, and analyzing data to gain valuable insights and inform decision-making.

2. The Data Science Process:

The data science process typically involves the following steps:

a. Data Collection:

Data collection is the first step in the data science process. Data can be sourced from various structured and unstructured sources, such as databases, CSV files, APIs, or even social media.

b. Data Cleaning:

Data collected from different sources may have inconsistencies, missing values, or errors. Data cleaning involves preprocessing the data to ensure it is accurate and reliable for analysis.

c. Data Exploration and Visualization:

Exploratory Data Analysis (EDA) involves visualizing and summarizing data to identify patterns and relationships. Data visualization tools like Matplotlib and Seaborn in Python or D3.js in JavaScript can help create insightful visualizations.

d. Data Analysis and Modeling:

In this step, various statistical and machine learning techniques are applied to analyze the data and build predictive models. Machine learning algorithms like Linear Regression, Decision Trees, Random Forests, and Neural Networks are commonly used in this phase.

e. Model Evaluation and Validation:

Once the models are built, they need to be evaluated and validated using metrics like accuracy, precision, recall, and F1-score. Cross-validation techniques are used to ensure the model's generalizability.

f. Model Deployment:

After successfully building and validating the models, they can be deployed to make predictions on new, unseen data. Model deployment can involve integrating the models into web applications, mobile apps, or other systems.

3. Introduction to Machine Learning:

Machine Learning is a subset of Artificial Intelligence that focuses on developing algorithms that enable computers to learn patterns from data and make predictions or decisions without explicit programming. There are three main types of machine learning:

a. Supervised Learning:

In supervised learning, the model is trained on labeled data, where the input and corresponding output are known. The goal is to learn a mapping from input to output so that the model can make predictions on new, unseen data.

b. Unsupervised Learning:

Unsupervised learning involves training the model on unlabeled data. The goal is to identify patterns or group similar data points without any predefined labels.

c. Reinforcement Learning:

Reinforcement learning is about training models to make decisions in an environment to maximize a reward signal. The model learns by interacting with the environment and receiving feedback on its actions.

4. Popular Data Science and Machine Learning Libraries:

There are several powerful libraries available in Python, JavaScript, and Ruby that make data science and machine learning more accessible and efficient. Some popular libraries include:

a. Python:

- Pandas: For data manipulation and analysis.

- NumPy: For numerical computations.

- Scikit-learn: For machine learning models and tools.

- TensorFlow and PyTorch: For deep learning models.

b. JavaScript:

- TensorFlow.js: A JavaScript library for training and deploying machine learning models in the browser.

- Brain.js: A library for neural networks and deep learning in JavaScript.

c. Ruby:

- Daru: A library for data manipulation and analysis in Ruby.

- SciRuby: A set of Ruby libraries for scientific and statistical computing.

5. Example of Data Science and Machine Learning Project:

Let's walk through a simple example of a data science project that involves predicting house prices based on features like square footage, number of bedrooms, and location using a machine learning algorithm.

1. Data Collection: Collect data on house prices and their corresponding features from real estate websites or APIs.

2. Data Cleaning: Clean the data by handling missing values, removing outliers, and encoding categorical variables.

3. Data Exploration: Visualize the data to understand the relationships between features and target variables.

4. Data Preprocessing: Split the data into training and testing sets for model evaluation.

5. Model Selection and Training: Choose a suitable machine learning algorithm (e.g., Linear Regression) and train it on the training data.

6. Model Evaluation: Evaluate the model's performance on the testing data using metrics like Mean Absolute Error (MAE) or Root Mean Squared Error (RMSE).

7. Model Deployment: Deploy the trained model to make predictions on new data, allowing users to get estimated house prices based on their inputs.

6. Conclusion:

Data Science and Machine Learning are powerful techniques that have the potential to transform businesses and industries by leveraging the power of data. In this chapter, we explored the data science process, introduction to machine learning, popular libraries, and an example project. By learning these concepts and tools, developers can harness the potential of data to gain valuable insights and make informed decisions.

CONCLUTION

In conclusion, "Basic Guide to Programming Languages: Python, JavaScript, and Ruby" aims to provide readers with a comprehensive understanding of programming fundamentals and the versatility of three popular languages - Python, JavaScript, and Ruby. Throughout the book, we have covered a wide range of topics, from basic concepts like variables and control structures to advanced subjects like data science and machine learning. Our goal was to equip readers with the knowledge and skills needed to embark on exciting programming projects and explore various applications of these languages.

We sincerely thank our readers for choosing this book as their guide on their programming journey. We hope that the content presented here has been valuable and that it has helped you build a strong foundation in programming. We understand that learning a new skill can be challenging, but your dedication and commitment to mastering programming concepts will undoubtedly pay off in the long run.

As you continue your programming journey, remember to practice regularly, work on real-world projects, and stay curious about new developments in the field. The world of programming is ever-evolving, and staying updated with the latest advancements will enable you to harness the full potential of these powerful languages.

We hope that this book has sparked your passion for programming and inspired you to explore even further. If you have any questions or need further guidance, don't hesitate to seek help from online communities, forums, and other resources.

Once again, we extend our heartfelt gratitude to all our readers for choosing "Introduction to Programming: Python, JavaScript, and Ruby." Your support means the world to us, and we wish you all the success in your programming endeavors. Happy coding!

THANK YOU!

www.ingramcontent.com/pod-product-compliance
Ingram Content Group UK Ltd.
Pitfield, Milton Keynes, MK11 3LW, UK
UKHW030622120125
4040UKWH00015B/415

9 781088 276426